A
PREACHER'S EPILOGUE

BRIAN THOMPSON

© Brian Thompson, 2024

Published by Brian Thompson

All rights reserved. No part of this book may be reproduced, adapted, stored in a retrieval system or transmitted by any means, electronic, mechanical, photocopying, or otherwise without the prior written permission of the author.

The rights of Brian Thompson to be identified as the author of this work have been asserted in accordance with the Copyright, Designs and Patents Act 1988.

A CIP catalogue record for this book is available from the British Library.

ISBN 978-1-7398902-2-3

Typeset and cover design by Clare Brayshaw

Prepared and printed by:

York Publishing Services Ltd
64 Hallfield Road
Layerthorpe
York YO31 7ZQ

Tel: 01904 431213

Website: www.yps-publishing.co.uk

To my amazing children Carolyn, Jonathan and Rachel whose talents, hard work and love for their families are a constant source of pride for me.

I believe most of this comes from my lovely wife and their mother Patricia whom we all miss dearly since her death in 2012.

CONTENTS

	Author Introduction	viii
Chapter 1	How Odd of God	1
Chapter 2	It's All About Change	5
Chapter 3	Wrestling Jacob	16
Chapter 4	Intriguing	24
Chapter 5	What's It All About Alfie?	35
Chapter 6	Trinity Sunday and Spatial Awareness	41
Chapter 7	Suppundra	51
Chapter 8	Question Time	54
Chapter 9	Yes God is Good	66
Chapter 10	The Cross: Tragedy and Triumph	78
Chapter 11	Called to be Saints	88

AUTHOR'S INTRODUCTION

Following the publication of my first two books of sermons, (Sermons in Stones and Inside the Preacher's Mind), someone asked me whether I was going to write a third. "No way," was my response. I pointed out the time and the effort involved – and the not inconsiderable expenditure of such a venture (and who wants to read old sermons anyway?)

Nonetheless ideas still came to me so for some odd reason I continued to write new sermons and revise older ones, knowing I would not preach them but could share some of them with friends. Gradually I changed my mind about the possibility of a third book. I had plenty of material which would easily pass on so this is how my "Preacher's Epilogue" came to be. My wish is that you will find plenty to provoke thought and to help you in your journey in faith. I also noticed that an early sermon in that first book was "A Pilgrim's Progress" and it seemed appropriate that what was in effect a prologue to my preaching career needed an epilogue to complete the circle.

Brian Thompson
Knutsford, August 2024

A
PREACHER'S EPILOGUE

CHAPTER 1

HOW ODD OF GOD

How odd of God ... to choose the Jews.
A protest banner at a recent election rally read
BANISH RELIGION
Its holders danced behind the television broadcaster trying to get free air time. Many people might not approve of their tactics but would sympathise with their message. In the light of Israel's attitude to Palestinians they could have been led to the opinion that a religion free world would be a happier place for us to live and grow up in. There are even some Jews who regret God's choice of them as a Chosen People.

In 1955, when I was a National Service man in Egypt, a colleague and I used some leave in order to visit Jerusalem and Bethlehem. We were offered a lift across the barren Jordan Valley by missionary friends who stopped their car outside a refugee camp for displaced Palestinians. We watched the long queues outside the high wire fence. Water was being distributed by United Nations Water Agencies.

Refugees were allowed out with buckets for their meagre supply of the essential liquid.

My friend Rhys and I both came to see that this whole situation needed urgent action if troubles in coming years were to be avoided. Promises were made but Jewish houses in many areas still appear and oppressed Palestinians, whose daily travel is restricted by "fences", remain very resentful of their treatment. FOR GOD'S SAKE Mr Netanyahu, how many more families will wake up tomorrow morning grieving for loss of loved ones because of what most of the world sees is a result of a policy of ethnic cleansing?

How many Israeli mothers will receive their returning soldier sons back home as lifeless corpses in body bags? How many innocent children will be condemned to a life of being disabled because their feet and legs have been damaged by your soldiers (and therefore with your approval)?

In the book of Daniel there is a graphic short story about writing appearing on the palace wall of the Persian king Balshazzar during one of his lavish feasts. The Jewish exiled prophet Daniel is summoned and he interprets the words as being a message from God. This modern reading from "The Message" by Eugene Peterson will make a startling impact on many of us:

"Listen O King! The High God gave your father Nebuchadnezzar a great kingdom and a glorious reputation.

You are his son...yet you are as arrogant as he ever was... You had the chalices brought by your father from God's Temple in Jerusalem to be used in your drunken party.

This is what the words on the wall mean: You have been weighed on the scales and don't weigh much... Your kingdom has been divided up and handed to the Medes and the Persians. That same night Balshazzar was murdered."

Dramatic and to the point! No offer of repentance. How odd of God. Further thought made me ask whether this incident in itself was an opportunity for a fresh start which the arrogant ruler missed.

When we Christians think about conversion we tend to use words like there being a way back to God through the dark paths of sin and a door which is open for all to go in. Entry is through the Cross and we are required to come as sinners to Jesus.

Many of us look back with joy and gratitude at such holy moments. But we must be aware that conversion is not a Christian prerogative. *All* religions lay claim to such moments of personal encounter with God. Where then in this story is the offer of a personal encounter and the failure to even recognise it? Is it, I wonder, in the warning about scales and God's generous suggestion of a way out? How many escape routes has God offered to Mr Netanyahu? For God's sake, Benjamin, think again – for your own sake, for your country, for Palestinians, for future generations of your two great nations, for the whole world. Unlike Balshazzar, LISTEN , and LEARN.

Is there anything we, ordinary church goers, can learn and pass on from the dreadful murder in Southport of young girls and the subsequent outbreaks of organised rioting in many towns and cities? Above all we must recognise that for every person with evil intentions there are hundreds of thousands who practise the power of good in their lives each day. Many of these come from all faiths and will acknowledge God as the source of all goodness and truth. We, plus all who do not believe in any God, have a joint responsibility as human beings to care for the world, for each other, for plants and animals, for the future. This has nothing to do with religion per se. It is a matter of sheer common sense. Simple!

In the recent election campaign the Labour Party cleverly chose a single word to define their mission. The word was CHANGE – which reminded me of a sermon I preached some years ago called "It's all about Change." I was attempting to show that becoming a Christian or going to a church puts you in a position of having to face changes. I will share a large part of this sermon with you so let me give it a chapter of its own.

CHAPTER 2

IT'S ALL ABOUT CHANGE

There is a game called STATIONS which we used to play at Sunday School parties and Chapel Socials in the church I grew up in (in Yorkshire) Maybe it was played in Cheshire too.

Plenty of space was required as the players sat down in a large circle of chairs.

Every seat was occupied but one person stood in the middle.

He or she was the train announcer.

Each player had been given the name of a station.

The game began when the announcer called out a route such as "Leeds to Scarborough changing at York." The three people with those station names then had to change places before the announcer could sit down on one of their chairs. Whoever was left standing then became the announcer and the game carried on with different routes and increasing activity.

Occasionally an announcer would shout "All change!" and *everybody* had to find a new seat- thus causing a frantic, chaotic mass movement, worse even than shopping at the Trafford Centre on a New Year Sale

Day! Actually I haven't yet experienced that (and am not likely to) but can imagine it because I once made the mistake of going with my wife to a Sale Day at the White Rose Centre in Leeds.

The game of stations made for some bizarre journeys, say Manchester to Morecambe via Cambridge and Cardiff.

The analogy could be drawn, I suppose, that each one of us is on a journey through life; and our journeys involve change.

Some changes are unplanned, taking us by surprise.

Some send us where we really don't want to go and *all* changes, pleasant or otherwise, bring measures of uncertainty and anxiety – the more so if our lives are not grounded in the confidence that we are loved by others, and therefore never alone.

Generally speaking human beings do not like change. We prefer the security of the settled and known ways –especially once we have left behind the exciting challenges of young days where we were beginning to discover what our future roles in life might be, which direction we were travelling in, what sort of people we were becoming, what friendships we were laying down, what contributions we could make to society, what was important to us, what our beliefs and rules for living were.

Ah! That turbulent and formative time of life, so adventurous, so risky, so precious!

Perhaps your memories (like mine) are a mixture: happy, wistful, with some regrets?

Perhaps you too are grateful that we came through the 16 to 30 stage unscathed, wiser and ready to accept the cosiness of a comfortable rut without the constant interruption of change after change, because change disturbs us.

Just over 20 years ago a highly respected American Bishop wrote a book with the title "Why *Christianity* must Change or Die"

It was a challenge to the Church in The United States but also had, and still has, important questions for the wider church to consider.

This morning I invite you to explore with me the role of change in the world and in the Church. I put it to you that as Christians our lives are built upon an unchangeable God who constantly calls us to make changes.

We sing hymn words such as:

"Change and decay in all around I see;
O thou who changest not, abide with me!"
"thou changest not, thy compassions they fail
not, as thou hast been thou for ever wilt be"

"Will you come and follow me if I but call your name? Will you go where you don't know and never be the same?"

We hear words of scripture such as:

"Jesus went to Galilee preaching the message of God; Time's up! God's kingdom is here! Change your life." (That's in Mark ch1.)

And in Romans 12, again using The Message version:

"Fix your attention on God. You'll be changed from the inside out... God brings the best out of you, develops well-formed maturity in you

If someone asks us "What is Christianity all about?" we could well reply "It's all about change." Or we could simply point our enquirer to the words of the Bryn Rees hymn about the Kingdom of God (Singing the Faith 255)

You will notice, especially through the verbs, the changes to our lives and to society which the kingdom or the rule of God brings:

"The K of G is justice and joy, for Jesus restores what sin would destroy"

In verse 2 there is good news for sinners because the Kingdom of God is mercy and grace. So we can expect freedom and a welcome – and the hope which will take away our feelings of despair. Nouns are introduced to show the results of the changes.

The Kingdom of God is challenge and choice the third verse tells us, involving us in repentance and that is hardly a passive move.

What is Christianity all about?" It's all about change.

So great is the change that faith in Christ brings to our lives that it can only be adequately described in the language used in stories and poetry, parables, metaphor – which is what Jesus often did when he was trying to make a point. And the gospel writers also did.

Concerning the message of change perhaps the best example is the story of the wedding in Cana of Galilee, the first of the miracles or signs which, according to the writer of John's Gospel, demonstrated the significance of Jesus.

This was the last of the written gospels, not appearing until some 60 years or so after the events recorded.

To accept this story word for word as actual history (as some people do) presents a number of problems. For instance it contradicts the account of Jesus's Temptations in which he firmly rejects the suggestion that he should use miraculous powers to win followers.

Secondly, if it all happened just as stated, why do the other gospel writers not include such an amazing occurrence in *their* accounts? (The same can be said, of course, of the raising of Lazarus). You might also wonder why Jesus's response to his mother is so abrupt.

In John's gospel the miracles of Jesus are called "Signs" because they demonstrate the significance of Jesus, the Jewish Messiah and the Saviour of the world. So this wedding, the opening scene of Jesus's public ministry, is saying "This is what this story of Jesus is all about."

"It's about the change that faith in Jesus can bring to your life and to the world – as effective and dramatic as water changing into new wine would be at a wedding party which was in trouble".

That is a metaphorical reading – one which asks us what the meaning of a story is and what it is saying to us today. I find this preferable to the purely literal approach and a useful way of looking at the Bible as a whole. The solely literal view can lead us into dead ends and convoluted explanations to unanswerable and unimportant questions.

Before closing I must return to my earlier proposition that as Christians in the 21st century, living in rapidly changing times, we are invited to put our trust in an unchangeable God who constantly calls us to make changes and to be his instruments of change.

Whenever discussion about change takes place many popular opinions are expressed. Two in particular I have to contest. One is when the phrase "The good old days" is used and the other is the outlook of the hymn writer with his words, "Change and decay in all around I see".

In many areas the good old days weren't all that good were they? Who wants to go back to days before sliced bread and heating and fitted carpets? Where would we be without worldwide air travel, mobile phones, microwave ovens, digital TV, computers and the internet – and teabags?

Rather than bemoaning change and decay modern hymn writers, (indeed all of us) would want to celebrate change *and progress*. Whilst acknowledging that not all change has been for the better mostly it has, and we must beware of wallowing in nostalgia and generalizing –though we all do it!

The changes we have lived through in our lives are bewildering but breathtaking. Our grandparents, if they could be teleported to us would be gob-smacked at all the changes in such a short time.

Take them to church (where it has been said "The wheels of God grind slowly") and they will be surprised by new things:

> modern translations of the bible, (What would they make of The Message version?),
>
> new hymns and songs (What happened to the old Methodist Hymn Book and Ancient and Modern?),
>
> words and pictures appearing on screens,
>
> music groups with singers and guitars!

They might also ask:

> "Why are some people raising their hands and where are the men's Sunday best suits and ladies' hats?
>
> "Where are the pews and the pulpit?"
>
> "Is that a *lady* minister? How did she get in?
>
> "What's going on?"

I think we would get a mixed reaction to church from our grandparents – and certainly from our great grandparents.

In his book the American Bishop points to changes not just in church buildings, furniture and worship but also in our traditional teaching about the Bible, the life of Jesus, the Creeds, all those theological issues which have been challenged by intense scholarly research over many years.

Under the spotlight too has come the church's attitude to scientific discoveries and medical advances – resulting in the many ethical issues society now faces in our modern age where Christianity in Britain is sidelined and church attendance is still in decline.

Do not lose heart though because the church has many great positives and many wonderful people. We have much to offer to society and the world.

Many Christians and most churches have shown a willingness to adapt to all the changes around us and to introduce new ideas. *Because* we are followers of Jesus we care about people and we look beyond our doors to wherever there is need, trying to extend a helping hand as well as experimenting with fresh expressions in worship styles and church organisation.

Regarding those big issues which are constantly in the news, such as Brexit, climate change, immigration, assisted dying and gay marriage, the Church can never speak with one voice. Christians, like everyone else, have differing opinions. But we can keep an open mind, whilst listening carefully and prayerfully to the experts, in our search for a Christian perspective.

It seems important that we set the example of Christian humility by being prepared to change our former views if necessary. This is not new. In fact the Church has a history of doing U-turns on entrenched attitudes. It started with the first century Council of Jerusalem deciding that Gentiles could become Christians without having to first accept the rites and regulations of the Jewish faith.

The abolition of the slave trade, the formation of the Trades Union movement, the overthrow of Apartheid, the running of food banks are all examples of the Church's role in making the world a better place.

God, it appears, would have us be his instruments of change.

All this is political because politics is about people and justice and equality and so is the Church. Therefore we cannot stand by silent on the sidelines. We must somehow or other provide a voice for those who have been rendered vulnerable and voiceless. Do we not regularly pray "Thy kingdom come, thy will be done *on earth*". There is much more to our beliefs and witness than the quest for personal salvation and a booked place in heaven!

Another hymn has the words "Nothing changes here." Sadly there will be aspects in the life of many churches where that could be hung as a banner. That is not a criticism but a challenge. I make an observation, (based on over 30 years in the classroom teaching Religious Studies in High Schools, as well as Sunday School and Youth work and preaching), that part of the reason why the church has failed to keep its young people is that, to them, the Church seems stuck in the past. Challenged by good education and modern science, they have found traditional Christian explanations and beliefs unsatisfactory.

Once a month I go to a U3A Philosophy Group a number of whom claim to be atheists. Deep thinkers but their ideas of what Christians believe are woefully mistaken. Within the Church itself there are sincere worshippers whose ideas about God have not developed since their Sunday School days. For them also, "nothing changes here."

Looking back over *your* Christian life, do you detect change or are you stuck with teaching about God and the Bible which you picked up as a child? The findings of modern scholarship taught in our training colleges have often not got through from pulpit to pew. So it is that many folk, even eminent scholars like Richard Dawking, assume that being a Christian requires you to believe that the Bible is infallible and without error; that Adam and Eve and a talking snake really existed; that Jesus walked on water and fed a huge crowd with a handful of bread and fish.

And of course all Christians are thought to accept that God is a stern Judge who looks down from somewhere in the distant heavens watching our every move and ready to condemn us to the eternal flames of Hell. All of which is a massive distortion of the true picture – it is fake news.

The message of John the Baptist and of Jesus to "Change your lives!" is at the heart of the gospel and as Christians we proclaim that it is *not* fake news. It is good news, which is what the word gospel actually means.

Commit your life to Christ and you will be changed. Of that there is no doubt. As we gradually surrender heart, mind and strength to Jesus he gives us new attitudes to others, new ways of living and thinking and doing and being.

Standing still in our faith is not an option. The process of change will not always be smooth. Sometimes there will be stops, starts and even reverses, but we must not give up because our unchangeable God beckons us It is a call to a life of change, of growing up, of progress.

Does not Charles Wesley have us sing about our being "changed from glory into glory" (a gradual process surely)

"till in heaven we take our place"?

That's in the future and not for us to worry about at this moment. But we might just go away today asking ourselves whether in our faith we are stuck in the past or maybe at a standstill.

"Change your ways!" therefore could well be a message for *you* – and for me.

Most of my recent written sermons have been from the early chapters of Genesis, for instance "Wrestling Jacob." In Jacob we come across a fascinating man who, I suggest needs a chapter of his own. Let's see what *you* make of Jacob.

CHAPTER 3

WRESTLING JACOB

There is a very strange story about Jacob in the depths of our Old Testament history – the days of the Hebrew Patriarchs . Abraham. Isaac, Jacob.

At times it is difficult to like Jacob, or Israel as he came to be known. It was not for nothing that from his childhood days he acquired the reputation of being a liar and a cheat. He was arrogant and manipulative. In our encounter with him this morning he even has the bare faced cheek to argue with God. Let's see what Jacob gets up to.

Genesis chapter 32vv24-32 in the New Revised Standard Version provides the details:

Jacob was left alone, and a man wrestled with him until daybreak. When the man saw that he did not prevail against Jacob, he struck him on the hip socket; and Jacob's hip was put out of joint as he wrestled with him. Then the man said, "Let me go, for the day is breaking." But Jacob said "I will not let you go, unless you bless me." So he said to him, "What is your name?" And he said, "Jacob". Then the man said, "You shall no longer be called Jacob, but Israel, for you have striven with God and with humans. Jacob called the place Peniel, saying "I have seen God face to face, and yet my life is preserved." The story ends at sunrise with Jacob limping away because of his damaged hip.

No doubt Jacob was left with unanswered questions and perhaps in need of paracetomols! – "What has just happened to me? Was it real, or just a very vivid dream?"

Today, over three millennia later, what do *we* make of it? Is this historically accurate, or folklore – or a mixture of both? And has it any relevance for us anyway? I venture to suggest that there are lessons to be learned from Jacob's obscure experience. Let's look for parallel circumstances in our own lives.

We all know, in differing degrees, what it is to wrestle with problems. And it's always much worse during the night isn't it? (You may, or may not, bring God into the equation. But please consider that perhaps He is always there, as many would affirm, just waiting for your invitation.)

Some of you might recall such a time recently – even last night. Disturbing worries keep us awake. Tossing and turning we emerge drained in the morning, perhaps to find that nothing has changed. Our anxieties remain though sometimes the door to a new resolve may be opening for us. That is my prayer for *you.*

Many people have discovered such resolve and conviction to be true. A few days ago in my home of residence I overheard a French lady, who has lived and worked in our country more than half of her life. She was commenting with conviction, "I am not a foreigner." I don't know the context of her conversation but it was not argumentative.

It was said after the recent SNP leadership election that Britain now has a Muslim leader, A Hindu head and maybe a Christian. I think that is cause for celebration – as well as an acknowledgement of the rapid and remarkable progress of the Black Lives Matter and other such movements. Christians especially, following the teachings and example of Jesus, should be careful not to use language which suggests that we are superior whilst others are less important to God.

Only the other week in the Laura Kuenssberg programme the Foreign Secretary used the term "these people" of asylum seekers. "These People"? Us and them? How divisive and condescending does that make us sound? We must not "other" people.

In God's world there are *no* foreigners. We are brothers and sisters in His one family and He loves each one of us irrespective of who we are and of what we have done.

In many churches it is now the custom at Communion services to have an "open table." We don't have to be a member, we don't even have to be a good person. "*All* are welcome at the Lord's Table," are the words of the invitation. That is the ideal and of course the Church has often fallen woefully short of her noble aims – and still does.

I wonder if you were disturbed recently by a report on the state of religion in the United Kingdom? This, I think, is the product of the National Statistics Office which comes out at regular intervals (Ten years or so).

There is no input from religious groups, which is right because they would want to influence the conclusions of honest outsiders. The unbiased opinion of the report was that based on current trends and the increasing number of elderly worshippers, it seems unlikely that the church and other groups like Sikhs and Muslims will continue to exist in their present form in ten years' time.

Questions such as; "Can we still call ourselves a Christian country?" arise. Is there anything we can do to address, or at least delay, this approaching death knell for our beloved Christian Church?

Well, that is one challenge I want to look at in this sermon and I would value your follow up input because we are all in this together.

How brave of our new king to open up the Palace records on the Crown's connections with profits from, and dealings with, slave traders. Who knows what an honest outside research will reveal and what past wrongs will be put right?

Has the time come for the same sort of self-examination and honesty, the same sort of spotlight, to be shone on the Church as a whole and on individual churches within the total body of Christ on earth? Another big question for us to consider.

One of my favourite writers and theologians is the American Brian McLaren. He belongs to what is known as Progressive Christianity, pioneered by Bishop Spong and Marcus Borg and hundreds more in America and Britain, Europe and now across the World. (Look it up on the internet).

Brian's latest book is called "Do I stay Christian?" In it he examines in great detail the question which many people in the Church are now asking: "In view of the possible forecasted demise of Christianity has the time come for me to desert the sinking ship and leave?" Disturbingly it is a question apparently being asked by many clergy, scholars and leaders. Why is there such disillusionment and how can we deal with it?

Brian McLaren tackles first this "Why?" question and as he delves into church history it is not an easy read for us because there is so much for us to be ashamed about.

In the early post resurrection days there was so much promise in this new vibrant movement. There are glimpses of this in the Acts of the Apostles and in the letters of Paul and others. Then in the early fourth century Emperor Constantine converted to Christianity and the Church's big mistake was that it kept in step with fading Rome's love of political power and as the Empire collapsed the Church took its place as the dominant power in people's lives.

Women played an important part in the early Church in roles of leadership, preaching and teaching. When men took over they soon put a stop to that. The priesthood became all male and women were very much side-lined – and still are with a few notable exceptions such as the Bishop of Dover.

How many women have a voice as bishops in the House of Lords? How many Church Councils have yet to reach a fair and equal representation of both sexes, in spite of the fact that without female input many churches would fall apart? Am I right?

In spite of everything we can be very proud of the Church's role in history. People looked at the early Church and marvelled at how much these followers of Jesus loved and cared for each other and how that spilled over. Wherever in the world there have been people in need the Church has stepped in to help.

In medical care, in education, in poverty, in warfare, in crises, in natural disaster there has been Church intervention and it still goes on and will continue. Our hearts and our pockets are touched because it is the right thing to do and for us who are Christian we are simply following the teaching of Jesus (Matthew 25v.31-40).

So then, be thankful for the Church and for your own particular church and for all the many blessings which come your way from Christian fellowship.

But let's get back to the disillusionment sensed by Brian McLaren and the question "Do we stay Christian?" Many chapters are devoted to the depressing history of Church failings. Gory details are not happy reading but perhaps they are necessary for us to know. You will be aware of some of our mistakes so I mention only a few. The Crusades and the slaughter of good, innocent Muslims to "rescue" Jerusalem is just a start. Colonisation and Empire building, imposition of Englishness on conquered lands, including religious worship, acquiring trading rights and valuable resources were to follow and the great evil of slavery. The Inquisition, the drowning of witches, the burning of bibles, the excommunication of scientists whose studies contradicted Church teachings and so it goes on from century to century and now includes sexual sins within the clergy. And all of that has caused some to sever their connections with the church. "Who can blame them?" is the question posed by our learned author.

It was with some relief for me that half way through his book Brian McLaren answered his question about whether to remain a Christian with a resounding "Yes!" (Chapter 15, page 159). He quotes another Progressive Christian writer. Diana Butler Bass. In her book *"Freeing Jesus"* she writes this: "When quizzed why I am still a Christian, I have always responded, "Because of Jesus. I know it sounds corny, but I love Jesus."

McLaren comments, "I feel the same way. Only Jesus provides a way for Christians to stay Christian....We love Jesus."

When I, (the lesser Brian here), faced up to the question of whether or not I should stay Christian I asked myself a very simplistic question about what I would miss most if I turned my back on the Church. The answer was the hymn singing. Methodists like me would agree. We sing our faith and in doing so we put ourselves in touch with Jesus, with God, with the Scriptures and with each other.

Brian McLaren's answer covers many chapters and is very detailed. He gives hundreds of reasons for his "Yes!" I guarantee that you will find them convincing.

As I reach the conclusion of this written sermon, (or response to current issues facing the Church), I reflect that we are in the Easter season and the words of Fred Pratt Green's hymn come to mind:

"The Church of Christ, in every age beset by change but Spirit –led, must claim and test its heritage and keep on rising from the dead." (Singing the Faith 415)

We are in a challenging but exciting age and certain issues lie ahead for our churches – but these are for another time and other brains perhaps. In the meantime we carry on without fear, reminding ourselves that ours is a Resurrection Faith and that not even the gates of hell could destroy Christ's Church.

Brian Thompson Knutsford Easter 2023
(Gospel story in Mark 7v.24-30 and Matthew 15v21-28. Worth looking at if this were a complete service.

Some pressing issues now facing churches: ageing and diminishing congregations, morale, caring for our ministers and leaders, attitudes to LGBT groups, assisted dying, outreach – on top of all our caring in the community and wider world. Wow! Who said that being a Christian was a cop out?

CHAPTER 4

INTRIGUING

Intriguing is a word that sums up my current dilemma as a Methodist Local Preacher at present unable to take services. Ideas still come, however, so I resort to writing sermons in the hope that at least a few friends might share my current thinking and thus be given an opportunity to agree, to disagree or simply to reject my views.

Reading the book "Jesus's Alternative Plan" by Richard Rohr has reminded me that a large part of the Gospel ministry of Jesus was devoted to healing – a fact which over my sixty years of preaching I am forced now to consider how well that has been reflected in my words from the pulpit.

I have often spoken about the miracles of Jesus, many of which ended in amazing cures, but how frequently have I linked this to the Church's wider Ministry of Healing? (and is it necessary to do that anyway?)

Part of my reluctance lies in the fact that two of my children are medics. They are quick to correct me if, in general conversation, I express an opinion which is medically incorrect. I have learned to be careful in what

I say, or write, and to be thankful for their superior knowledge.

Another bit of my reluctance comes from the modern scientific tendency to rationalise the miracles of Jesus. But we cannot get away from the fact that the Gospels make it very clear that "Jesus went round the whole of Galilee, teaching in their synagogues, proclaiming the good news of the Kingdom of God and curing all kinds of illness and disease among the people." (Matthew 4v23). Unbiased writers at the time, such as the Jewish historian Josephus, do not contradict this.

Two Bible readings to accompany this sermon are Luke 7v 11-17 and II Kings 4v8-36. Both describe healing miracles in the village of Nain in Galilee. Several centuries separate the bringing back to life of two young men who were also the only sons of grieving widows.

Is there a happy coincidence here, or some deliberate planning? Was Luke using his writer's poetic licence for dramatic literary effect? I can't work it out. Maybe you will share your ideas.

Luke's drama has Jesus interrupting a funeral procession by touching the wicker basket bier on which the corpse was carried (and still is in Middle Eastern countries). For Jesus, a Jew, physical contact with the dead was a very serious breach of religious and cultural protocol which could lead to complicated ritual cleansing, rejection by local community and synagogue and temporary isolation from friends – even worse than our own experience of Covid lockdowns.

Permit me to digress for a moment. In my younger days, when I was just starting out as a very raw preacher, it was generally thought that Methodists were required to be strictly teetotal – maybe having to "Sign the Pledge" and avoid entering a pub. My church even retained an annual Temperance Sunday service when an invited preacher would address us with a boring lecture on the evils of alcohol.

I used to imagine that a suitable text for such a sermon could be found in the story of the funeral procession in Nain when Jesus broke all the rules by touching the coffin, or bier as it was called. Picture a temperance preacher beginning the sermon with the words: "My text is a warning to KEEP OFF THE BEER!"

Another little spelling/pronunciation quirk appeared during my research for all this. I wonder why teetotaller begins with t double e. Wouldn't t-e-a be more appropriate?

But my digression has gone on too long, indicating my butterfly mind and my confusion as to where I go next. Forward is the only way of course. The real comfort for all Christians is that we are always on a shared journey into the future and, as St Paul reminds us, that all things work together for good when we love God" (Rom 8v28)

If this sermon were ever to reach a pulpit it would need at least one suitable hymn.

The words "So every day we're on our way for we're a travelling, wandering race, we're the People of God.. (Singing the Faith 473).

I thought this was ideal but then I realised it involved so much repetition and takes too long to sing anyway. There must be some fitting modern hymns but I leave others to research this. What I do notice is that the central doctrine of pilgrimage seems to be getting discarded. The Methodist Hymn Book of 1933 contained a section of 35 hymns under the heading "Pilgrimage, Guidance Perseverance." Singing the Faith does not make our search any easier. So I turned back to the early hymnal because bits of "Through the Night of Doubt and Sorrow" were coming to mind – and I like the tunes suggested! I share with you some of what I think are the more relevant points to consider today from this hymn copyrighted in 1915.

Through the night of doubt and sorrow. We all know those moments do we not and it is often during the night when they disturb us the most. The world seems such an unhappy place these days and our prayers become more difficult and even angry.

WHY? Is the repeated question we all ask at times and it seems that no answers are given.

I can safely say that every reader and listener will have agonised with the WHY question and maybe even at this moment are grappling with it. Various reasons may be at the root of your troubles such as a serious health issue, the death of a friend or family member, a broken relationship, loss of employment, money problems....

Our hymn suggests in many places that help and comfort are to be found in having faith in God's absolute love for each one of us.

In our search for answers are there lessons we can learn from the old Negro Spirituals? The suffering slaves sang their "songs of expectation". Though they remained in cruel bondage they found a different kind of freedom which was denied to their slave-masters.

John Bunyan's voice from a prison cell in Bedford (where in 1684 he wrote "The Pilgrim's Progress") echoes this freedom in the suggestion that no discouragement can make a Christian relent his or her first vowed intent to be a pilgrim.

We rightly modernise our language but please let us never forget that we, followers of Jesus in the 21st century have joined him along a pilgrim way which began when this humble workman from Galilee called a few disciples to be Fishers of Men.

It was with that call that the Church's foundations were laid some twenty centuries ago – which means that we do not travel alone. We have been given the privilege of being part of this world wide family of the Master and his Friends – the Church of Jesus.

Whenever we worship we remind ourselves of several things:

> that God is always with us;
>
> that the Church spans the globe
>
> that we are meant to be forward moving and filled with faith and hope
>
> that the journey has a destination promised by Jesus and will not just fizzle out.

These guarantees made by Jesus after he had washed the feet of his disciples are the bedrock of Christian belief and practice.

"Do not let your hearts be troubled. Believe in God, believe also in me. In my Father's house there are many dwelling places. If it were not so, would I have told that I go to prepare a place for you? And if I go and prepare a place for you, I will come again and will take you to myself, so that where I am, there you may be also." (From John 13 and 14 NRSV)

"Jesus with us all the time!" Better still is our hymn's suggestion, "Brother clasps the hand of brother stepping fearless through the night." Another hymn refers to us as a happy band of pilgrims. How can we be other than happy if we have Jesus and countless Christians as our fellow travellers?

My previous church in Leeds made the decision to stop our practice of sending Christmas cards to every church member. We reasoned that important as Christmas is, Easter is even more important for Christians. WE ARE EASTER PEOPLE. Difficult as the resurrection is for us to understand, and even more difficult for us to explain to others, is it not the case that when we in grief attend the funeral of a friend or loved one we can still sing quietly but with deep inner confidence words such as:

*"Thine be the glory risen, conquering Son......
endless is the victory Thou o'er death has won.....
Lo. Jesus meets us risen from the tomb; lovingly he
greets us, scatters fear and gloom.......no more we*

doubt thee Glorious Prince of Life. Life is nought without thee, aid us in our strife...? (Singing the Faith 313)

Back to the issue of healing by Jesus and within the ministry of the Church which have exercised my mind and still do. I see within my own body miracles of modern medicine and am grateful beyond words for our amazing National Health Service. I sometimes feel like a spare parts person who has been rescued by the skills of doctors. After umpteen operations I walk around with two replacement knees, a pacemaker and a special stent down my chest. I have survived a heart attack and a twisted bowel. Any remaining difficulties are put down to old age!

Did Boris Johnson and friends really make those reported comments about old people being surplus to requirements and a drain on the economy? Even if said in jocular mode I for one do not intend to throw the towel in easily. I reckon there are plenty of other "old codgers" who will carry on trying to be useful, offering their wisdom and advice and being awkward when necessary.

Did you notice the description of the widow's son's healing in the second book of Kings; how Elisha applied mouth to mouth resuscitation. It reads like an extract from a modern first aid manual. Should we be surprised?

What does surprise me after all my brushes with health issues is that I am still here and being blessed. I really am nothing out of the ordinary and certainly not deserving of any special favours from God or human beings.

That's another WHY question for me to ponder. Why is the "heart of the eternal most wonderfully kind?" The answer lies somewhere in his love for each human being. An exciting topic for us all to delve into.

I started with Richard Rohr's Book on the Sermon on the Mount and in concluding I return to the eminent scholar's thought provoking masterpiece.

My daughter has placed a notice on the back of the door to my flat which says in large letters HEARING AID! because I have been known to venture out without this useful equipment. The thought occurs to me that perhaps words of Richard Rohr could be displayed to remind me of my responsibilities as a Christian out there in the real world. I browsed through his first pages and came up with these:

"The cross has still not been emptied of its power to transform human history."

"Jesus believes that God is a Person to be imitated, enjoyed and loved....It is all about relationship. All real living is meeting.

That simple and totally available experience makes all the difference." (so open your door Brian and meet people and you might find yourself meeting Jesus as well).

"Jesus tells us that God is totally accessible, that God is available in reality itself, in experience, in graced relationships. The reign of God is in our midst" (Luke 17v21).

Notices on the back of house doors are one way to remind us of important jobs and duties. On the doorposts of Jewish homes you will find a mezuzah. This is small box containing a parchment with the words of the SHEMA, their main prayer from Deuteronomy 6v.4 (Hear O Israel the Lord is our God and is to be loved with all our heart, mind and strength). The assurance being given is that God's blessings are theirs as they go out, as they return, and on all their comings and goings in life.

Looking for a way to end this sermon I turned to the writings of St Paul for ideas. I was struck by his comments on boasting in 2 Corinthians 11v.16-30.

I had wrestled hard and long as to whether I should include the personal details of my health struggles. Preachers are prone to be too reluctant to talk about themselves but very occasionally I reckon it is alright to be more open about our own concerns as well as our hopes. Let people into our lives so that we can "bear one another's burdens" (Galatians 6v2.) My decision to go ahead without alteration may be the wrong one. If so I can only apologise and learn from any criticism which comes my way.

My written sermons have a very limited readership of friends and preachers many of whom, like me, will have experienced the death of loved ones. Such times are almost impossible to bear without the support of family and friends. Most religions have coping rituals. I found help from the sermons of Peter Marshall and C.S.Lewis's "The Last Battle." Perhaps I can draw my thoughts to a conclusion by pointing to the former writer's sermon "The Problem of Falling Rocks." Marshall has been describing how the oyster deals with the irritating grain of sand by slowly covering it with a milky substance from which a precious pearl is eventually formed.

I quote the author's words: "The oyster has learned – by the will of God – to turn grains of sand into pearls, cruel misfortunes into blessings, pain and distress into beauty."

And that is the lesson we are to learn along this pilgrim way.

The grace of God, which is sufficient, will enable us to make of our troubles the pearls they can become.

Remembering the Mezuzah, doors are important for practising Jews.. A door features in "The Last Battle" and other Narnian tales. Going through you find that the inside is bigger than the outside – a bit like the Tardis, but sorry Dr Who fans, C.S. Lewis got there first. Peter Marshall, drawing on the Book of Revelation, says that we enter Heaven through Pearly Gates (or Doors) and every pearl is a trouble, a pain, a heartache, a misfortune which, by the grace of God, has been changed into a beautiful, lovely thing.

The concluding words of "The Last Battle" are these:

"Now at last they (the children of Narnia) were beginning Chapter One of the Great Story which no one on earth has read; which goes on for ever; in which every chapter is better than the one before."
And these must be my final words too.

WARNING: There is enough material in this chapter to cover several sermons and if ever it reached a pulpit I would use a whole month of services. Neither I nor a congregation have the stamina to endure all this in one go!!

CHAPTER 5

WHAT'S IT ALL ABOUT ALFIE?

Have any of you, I wonder, seen the Michael Caine classic film with its accompanying song "What's it all about Alfie?"

You are probably singing that in your head now.

If any of you respond to the name Alfie do not worry because I am not going to say anything uncomplimentary about Alfies.

We even had a king called Alfred and we dubbed him with a title – Alfred the Great. It's just that I want to use some of the song's words as the starting point for our thoughts.

If a friend were to look at your church-going habit and ask you why you do it: "What's it all about?" how would you reply? Would you point to the life of Jesus and his continuing influence on people's thinking and doing today; (quite remarkable some two millennia after he walked this earth); would you share your experiences of the richness of your church fellowship and the bonds of friendship you enjoy there; would you search your memory for a single bible verse to launch your argument?

If you choose the last of those options you would probably be looking for a verse from the Gospels or the letters of say Paul or John. Right? So you may be puzzled by my choice which is from the Old Testament book of the Prophet Micah. Hear his words from chapter 6 verses 6 to 8 in the New Revised Standard Version:

"With what shall I come before the Lord and bow myself before God on high? Shall I come before him with burnt offerings, with calves a year old? Will the Lord be pleased with thousands of rams, tens of thousands of rivers of oil? Shall I give my firstborn for my transgressions, (the fruit of my body for the sin of my soul?) He has told you, O mortal, what is good. And what does the Lord require of you but to do justice, and to love kindness, and to walk humbly with your God?"

Three requirements: justice, kindness, trusting in God (or walking humbly before him). What a brave announcement for the prophet to make, what a massive condemnation of the nation's system of sacrificial worship. Micah's words must have been heard with grave disapproval by the powerful religious leaders and would have put Micah himself in great personal danger.

Turning to the New Testament, are there any comparable Bible passages which sum up what God might suggest to modern Christians are his requirements for our beliefs and behaviour. Lots of choice and you will no doubt refer me to the teaching of Jesus in his parables and in the Sermon on the Mount. I refer you instead to Paul's letter to the Romans chapter 12 which is a very concise summary in line with the way we have been dealing with scripture so far. Let's hear it read now and be sure to read it later, and often, for further reflection.

READING: ROMANS CHAPTER 12 vv 9 –21
This is like an exercise in panning for gold. There are many words here but we sift out the mud or sand and dispose of the unwanted water back into the stream in our search for glistening pieces of the precious metal. There are plenty so I choose just a few. For instance:

Love one another with mutual affection
Hold fast to what is good
Do not lag in zeal
Rejoice in hope
Persevere in prayer
Bless those who persecute you
Weep with those who weep
Overcome evil with good

There is enough material in this chapter for a sermon for every Sunday in the year and more.

Paul it seems has the ability to get to the point and not to complicate his message with waffle, unlike some modern politicians and some sermons, including my own, where large chunks could be scored out with a single word in capital letters "SIMPLIFY."

Mischievously I wonder whether new members of parliament are given lessons on how to answer, (or not to answer), questions put to them by the media and the public? I can imagine advice such as:

"If it's a very awkward question never give an immediate answer, but use a delaying response such as, "Well, look!". Not many, but at least a few, fall into that trap. Thankfully most politicians are honest with us and win our approval no matter which party they represent. MPs need our prayers, for their job is vital – and virtually impossible without outside support.

A friend from Leeds came across as our guest to the recent RHS Flower Show at Tatton Park. It was a very, very wet day but we hired a wheel chair and went round the whole showground. I was able occasionally to push the wheel chair myself. The rain eased off in the afternoon. We eventually returned home reflecting on what a beautiful day's experience we had enjoyed together and one hopefully we can repeat in future years. We are all blessed by the outside help from others and should frequently ask ourselves "Who has been a support for me to-day and for whom have I been a blessing?"

But back to the question I put to you at the start: "What's it all about?" It would be unfair of me to fob that off on to you and leave it there. Easy for preachers to do, but if I pose a question to *you* then I have a responsibility to explain how I would respond. You are grown up enough in the faith to reach your own conclusions. My experiences may or may not help but I share them anyway because *we are fellow travellers on the Christian Road and have a lot to learn from each other*. So Brian Thompson: "What's it all about for you, all this church and God business? Well, I've bitten the bullet now haven't I? So here goes. Let's hope I do not choke!

Let me first say that I do not know all the answers – very few actually. As I get older I find I know less about matters of faith such as doctrines and there is an increasing reluctance for me to say "This I know!" Methodist Local Preachers are faced with an annual question as to whether we are faithfully preaching the teachings of the Methodist Church. Whoops! I may get thrown out on that one. Remember that Christianity is all about change. Obviously we do not expect to have the same beliefs and ideas we picked up in Sunday School. Ours is a faith which asks questions and invites us to adjust our understanding in the light of what we learn. An important point for me then in this self- examination is that I am still learning, still asking questions, still praying, still making mistakes. I may lose the plot from time to time but I am not losing faith in God and my admiration and love for Jesus is growing stronger as the days and years roll by.

Certain things help me. You too will have your own aids. My love of hymns as well as the scriptures and books by Christian authors such as Brian McLaren are all an inspiration. Well look (!) I am getting tired of talking about me and it must be boring for you so let me round off my "What's it all about for me?" task with a few afterthoughts.

"What's it all about Alfie? " is a question you and I have to each answer for ourselves. Why do we continue the habit of going to church, believing in God, living our lives in the way we do? Are the message and words of Jesus, St Paul, and the prophets, or the lyrics of many hymns or Beethoven's Ode to Joy any help or does our inspiration for living lie elsewhere as well?

This is a personal challenge which is why coming to church is a challenging and dangerous habit. One day God may really get through to you or me and ask " OK Alfie (put your own name there) what's it all about, what are you doing, are you prepared to give me your full attention and give me a chance with your life? (Inviting our and Isaiah's response: "Here am I, send me, use me").

I love churches with all their faults and yet have not explored this. A new sermon would be required but I think another writer would be preferable. Questions such as how we see the future of our church in fifty years' time in view of the continuing decline in numbers could be tackled.

I finish with more advice from St Paul: Philippians 4v8 "Whatever is true, whatever is honourable, whatever is just, whatever is pure, whatever is pleasing, whatever is commendable, if there is anything excellent and if there is anything worthy of praise, think about these things… and the God of peace will be with you ,"

May that be true for you, and you, and you, and me. In the days ahead and in all our lives may we find God's peace. AMEN

CHAPTER 6

TRINITY SUNDAY AND SPATIAL AWARENESS

Sometimes I think that I suffer from a lack of spatial awareness – or is it that by nature I am clumsy, with a tendency to bump into things? I remember at our wedding reception knocking over my wine glass as I stood up to give my speech. It could have just been nerves but on other occasions since the same thing has happened. I misjudge the height of the glass and over it goes! Rather embarrassing!

Also I have been known to trip up when climbing stairs or walking on the level. When eating out at a self-service cafe I may ask a companion to carry my food and drinks to the table. I have to be careful (*poor old fella*) to avoid catching the sound of a familiar and much missed voice which used to say, "Pick your feet up!" which if you think about it, is impossible to do anyway. It's like the old Yorkshire saying, "Frame thissen lad!" Can't be done but we know what it means. When I'm putting beakers into the cupboard I often fail to lift them high enough and bump them into the shelf or knock them onto the floor, which is not a good idea in a tiled kitchen.

Out of interest I looked up spatial awareness on Google, and I think I'm OK actually. People who really suffer walk into walls or off pavements. They don't drive because they can't judge the width of gaps and have difficulty parking. Revolving and sliding doors can be a challenge to them. No worries there for me but when I read about their problems with putting on duvet covers and trying to fit a wrong sized lid on a jar I recognise myself and stop researching. Too much knowledge after all can be a disturbing thing!

But why was I doing this anyway? Let me explain. These thoughts about space came to me as I was reading a fascinating theology book . Here it is: "The Divine Dance" by an American scholar and Franciscan priest, called Richard Rohr. It's all about the Trinity – the Christian understanding of the mystery of God as Father, Son and Holy Spirit; Three in One and yet One in Three and how they relate to each other – and more importantly how they relate to us.

At various points in the book the author explores the concept of space from a religious perspective. There is of course much more to space than we get from a physical view alone, which leads us to think of space as empty gaps between objects. Through the eyes of faith we may come to see that space can have deep spiritual meanings. Space is never just a pointless void. It can be, and perhaps always is, God occupied – filled with the glory of God.

I think that there is plenty of evidence in our scriptures and in the religious experience and practice of saints both old and new, famous and unknown (just like us), to encourage a personal search for our own spiritual spatial awareness, which will also reveal to us where we *lack* that sort of spatial awareness. This can be a humbling experience – a painful part of the learning process which helps us to be better followers of Jesus.

Such is the aim of this and of many a sermon. If that sounds daunting, do not worry because the challenge to make progress in your faith is *always* rather fascinating – so listen up!

I want us to consider three types of space. Let's start with the most obvious – familiar to all of us. When I say "space" most of you will immediately think of *outer* space: the vast beyondness of the universe. Perhaps you are a Star Trek addict or a science fiction fan, your imagination being fed by the great number of films and television series. Sound and visual effects make them much more vivid than my boyhood Saturday afternoon viewings of Flash Gordon at the Picture House, Pudsey, or the novels by HG Wells and Jules Verne which I borrowed from Bramley Library in Leeds.

The recent total eclipse of the sun, best seen from coast to coast across the United States, was not only witnessed direct by maybe 12 million Americans but also beamed around the world by television satellite. I guess that never before in the whole of history have so many people gazed up at the skies with exclamations of delight and wonder. Many regarded it as a spiritual experience, sharing the awe and worship of the psalmist. Listen to this:

Psalm 19 "The heavens are telling the glory of God; and the firmament proclaims his handiwork."

Psalm 8 "When I look at your heavens, the work of your fingers, the moon and the stars that you have established; what are human beings that you're mindful of them, mortals that you care for them?"

Hearing those words always reminds me of guard duties in Egypt as a young soldier, supposed to be watching for possible intruders through the barbed wire fences, but unable to block out my amazement at the star filled heavens and the shining radiance of the moon, especially when full. Even at 3 in the morning one could never feel cut off from God and all alone.

If you have doubts about the existence of God and are looking for evidence then the psalm writer's advice is a pretty good place to start. Consider the heavens, the moon and the stars. None of us can prove God but we can each attempt to catch glimpses of the mystery of his being.

Joseph Addison, a 17th century clergyman, wrote a hymn which begins:

*"The spacious firmament on high,
With all the blue ethereal sky,
And spangled heavens, a shining frame,
Their great Original proclaim.
The unwearied sun from day to day,
Doth his creator's power display..."*

Majestic words but we don't sing that hymn now because the second verse assumes the church teaching at the time that the earth was the centre of the universe with the sun going round it. Science has proved otherwise. It's the earth that moves round the sun. Addison was a child of his time and probably had his doubts even though he lived in an age of mistaken conceptions. But it's his conclusion that I miss. Surely we could all agree with his final conviction in the third and last verse where he has the stars and the planets rejoicing:

"They utter forth a glorious voice,
For ever singing as they shine:
THE HAND THAT MADE US IS DIVINE!"

Consider the heavens then and outer space and you may have to conclude, without being required to understand or to explain it all, that "the hand that made us is divine." When we contemplate the vastness and beauty of the heavens and beyond, like the awestruck psalmist we can see that here is an invitation to become more aware of God in our daily living.

Let's look for the next step in our quest for this vital spatial awareness. Again we turn to this Psalms for evidence:

The opening of Psalm 23 –
"The Lord is my shepherd, I shall not want. He makes me lie down in green pastures; he leads me beside still waters; he restores my soul."

The twenty third psalm is the world's favourite, loved by Jews and Christians worldwide, coming alive when read or sung at funerals and weddings. Learned by some of you at school you can probably recite it word for word. Why is it so well known and loved? Well, its simplicity and flowing poetry must be one reason but also, as one bible commentary puts it,

"it expresses more vividly than any other portion of scripture the individual's private experience of God's grace." (Daily Bible Study)

David, the author of this psalm, had cared for flocks of sheep from his boyhood. Now as King of Israel he was shepherd of his people, and he remembers lessons learned earlier. He is saying "Actually the Lord is *my* shepherd (and he is your shepherd too). He provides my needs so that I want for nothing. He looks after me, he leads me to the best pastures. The refreshing streams and still waters calm me. Resting in his care and love my fears are gone and my soul, my whole being, is restored so that I am at peace."

Isn't that what we all desire, long for – inner peace, tranquility? "Come to me all you that are weary and are carrying heavy burdens," said Jesus, "and I will give you rest" "Do not worry," was his repeated advice. We hear all this and we sing about it in our hymns. We believe it to be true but we are not very adept at putting it into practice are we? Sometimes we are like pedestrians on a railway or airport escalator continuing to carry our cases when we could easily just put them down for a moment.

"Cast all your anxieties on God," says the First Letter of Peter, "because he cares for you."

We could go on quoting scriptures for hours for there are hundreds of verses telling us to trust in God, to "wait upon him" – which means to contact him, to pray, to create an inner space for him to occupy, for it seems to be difficult for him to enter uninvited. He will not invade our personal space.

We all need our personal inner spaces. That's one reason why we come to church. In worship we open up to God and he often gets through to us. But of course we don't leave him in the building when we exit the doors. He is as close to us on Monday morning as much as on Sunday, and throughout our busy week with all its challenges and tensions he is by our side waiting for our invitation.

Now, so far in our search for *spiritual* spatial awareness we have thought about outer space and we've touched on inner space. What other sort of space is left? There must be a third point because that's how sermons often seem to work. Well there is and you will be glad to know it is brief, though not uncomplicated. Richard Rohr calls it "The Space Between."

This was new to me. Remember that this book *(The Divine Dance)* is about the Holy Trinity. In it the author suggests that there is a danger of trying to over define the Trinity. Preachers on Trinity Sunday may use their three points to explain the work of the Creator Father, the role of the Redeemer Son and how the Holy Spirit operates. Perhaps they will produce a diagram of a triangle or a picture of a clover leaf. Richard Rohr thinks there is a danger of Something being lost in this type of treatment. *That something* is the space between the Three.

He uses a metaphor which most parents will fondly relate to. When little ones are put to bed they can't always get to sleep easily. Sometimes, even in the middle of the night, using every excuse they can, they will crawl into your bed between the two of you. They now have all the safety and tenderness they crave. They have the best of both of you. Resting in that space, reaching out to touch both parents, they snuggle down in total security. There's something special in that for the parents too. The two adults are independent but the introduction of a third, the child, adds something novel to the mix. After kicking you in the kidneys you gently return them to their own beds – still asleep. The magic has worked!

The lesson drawn is this: that the most important element of the Trinity (Father, Son and Holy Spirit) is in their *relationship*, rather than in their separate identities. In one sense the Three are inseparable. Their relationship, their community is what really counts and the flow between them and from them is what the author calls "The Divine Dance". Furthermore it is a Dance which we are invited to join.

A final illustration from Richard Rohr may help us to understand that invitation. He shares with us his love of devotional religious art and his favourite icon painted by the Russian iconographer Andrei Rublev in the 15th century.

It is based on the very ancient story in Genesis chapter 18 of how "the Lord" appeared to Abraham in the form of "three men" (or were they angels? Or something even more?) Anyway Abraham and his wife welcome them and provide a fine meal. They don't join their guests but stand nearby under a tree to observe. They see in this incident a divine visitation, and a place at God's table is too much to hope for.

The icon was given the title "The Hospitality of Abraham" but is also called "The Trinity." The original hangs in a gallery in Moscow. Richard Rohr has a copy in his room. He is struck by the gaze between the three characters, showing their mutual respect for each other as they share the meal.

After the death of a minister friend of mine his wife Jill asked me if I would like to have a miniature of the icon which Graham kept on his desk. It's here on the communion table. Feel free to examine it after the service.

Richard Rohr is also intrigued by the hand of one of the three figures which points to the open fourth place at the table. Is this a foretaste of the Trinity right at the beginning of the Bible? "In the beginning was the Word" John's Gospel proclaims. If this story and this icon are right in their portrayal of the mystery of God's Being could we not equally say "In the beginning was the Relationship?" Are we seeing here a preview of Father, Son and Holy Spirit – Three in One and One in Three?

There is yet something more, for when the icon is examined more carefully there appears to be a small, rectangular hole at the front of the table. Art historians say this may be an indication that perhaps originally a mirror was fixed there – something unheard of in iconography. Perhaps it is saying that the empty place at the table is for the observer. You and I can look into the mirror and see ourselves there; for God's invitation and welcome is to all!

Yes, even *we* can know the love and the companionship of God; even *we* can join the dance and experience the Divine Flow in creation, in the world of human affairs, and within our own lives day by day.

Whenever we pray the benediction and whenever we think about the Trinity what power are we tapping into?

May the blessing of God the Father, God the Son and God the Holy Spirit be with us all in the week ahead and for evermore. AMEN

(Preached at Wesley Road Chapel, Armley, Leeds on the 27th May 2018)

CHAPTER 7

SUPPUNDRA

Somewhere in the library of sermons on my computer file is one with the title "Words, Words, Words." On my desk is a hard copy which has not yet reached a pulpit.

Writing sermons during the Covid lock-downs (as I did) kept my brain active and helped to preserve both my sanity and my faith. My stock of unpreached sermons has increased – which some might think is a waste of time and computer space and paper where I printed hard copies. Such opinions are probably right on all counts. "Words, words, words!" Waste of time?

My starting point here was a teacher's comment on my school report when I was eleven years old. "Conduct Good usually, but given to talkativeness at times."

Looking back on my 33 years career in teaching, and a period of preaching which spans over 60 years, I have to wonder whether my form master's words were far sighted and prophetic or just cruelly cynical – albeit an accurate summary of me at the time.

"Given to talkativeness!" Hey? (Interrupt me with your opinion in, say, two hours' time.)

But....All those lessons, all those school assemblies, all those sermons – words, words, words, and yet more words.

A few years ago I was having trouble with my voice and had to come off the preaching plan for a while. My son made the observation, "Perhaps God is saying something to you Dad!"

If so, God was not speaking loudly enough or I was not listening hard enough; anyway I carried on churning out more words in yet more sermons.

Actually I enjoy words and investigating not only what they mean but where they come from. And I love coming across new words.

When my son was at medical school he told me that his training would involve acquiring some thirty thousand new words. It's the same, to a greater or lesser extent, in any academic discipline isn't it? Training to be a motor mechanic or a rocket scientist involves disciplined study which is rewarding as you master new skills and knowledge.

Perhaps that is why I love theology because even after years of delving deeply into it, reading not only the scriptures but also the opinions and wisdom of many preachers and scholars, I find there are always new truths and fresh wonders to be discovered and taken on board – and shared.

I said that I love finding new words. The title of this sermon is SUPPUNDRA. I guess that's a new word for you, as it was for me.

What I am trying to do in this sermon is to point out the influence and the power of words – for good or for harm – in people's lives, in society and in the world. This I suggest is especially relevant for those who profess an interest in or a faith in God. Scripture points the way time and again.

(At this point on my computer my notes end so I must have accidentally deleted the rest. I remember quoting a prayer referring to Jesus as the Living Word and the Bible as God's Written Word and their relevance to our faith).

Now comes confession time. I hope you have not spent too long looking up lists of Indian Test cricketers or reading Asian Restaurant menus. There is no such word as suppundra. I invented it! Perhaps my attempted deception has no place in a Christian sermon but I wanted you to realise how much influence even false words have on us.

So my apologies! That is written sincerely.

Preachers are conveyors of "God's Spoken Word" What a privilege, and what a responsibility that brings. Maybe that is why the initial response to such a calling is often "No thanks God." Remember though that when God calls God will provide. (Jehovah Jireh – Genesis 22:14)

CHAPTER 8

QUESTION TIME

A preaching task I have recently set myself is to give my sermons titles which are the same as those of television programmes.

It's a gimmick which hopefully will capture the attention before the switch off mode descends on the captive audience, some of whom are bound to be pre-occupied.

The idea is to briefly mention the programme chosen and then try to show that sometimes links may be found between its title and a Christian theme or a Bible story.

For instance I've preached about *Neighbours, Tales of the Unexpected, Songs of Praise* and you'll hear another one in a few moments, if you're still awake.

There are others in the pipeline which may or may not come to fruition. Whirring around in my disorganised brain are programmes like *Loose Women* and *Men Behaving Badly* because there are plenty of examples of both within our scriptures, especially the wayward behaviour of (wait for it!) – men. If I were to preach on those words of Jesus in Matthew 6v19-20 about storing up for ourselves treasures in Heaven then perhaps I could begin with *Cash in the Attic*, (...Cash in the Attic... Treasures in Heaven) though some might think that to be too irreverent and flippant.

Pointless is another possibility. (I wonder if the Prodigal Son had reached that conclusion- pointless – about his own life which led him to "come to his senses" and return home?

Maybe *The Weakest Link* could introduce an exploration of the character of Judas Iscariot And if a sermon is required to look at the saga of Noah and the Ark isn't there a TV series about *Animal Rescue?*

All this is gimmicky maybe but it's really about stretching the imagination (or twisting it outrageously!) which is after all what Jesus did in his parables in order to make his point.

How many of you sometimes tune into *Question Time?* It's on too late of course but can be compelling and also very irritating. I suppose it depends who is on the panel and how often they appear. During those dreadful Brexit debate days I often thought, "Oh No! Not him again!" Other panellists too can cause me to respond in a most unchristian way. It's quite ridiculous to find myself shouting "Rubbish!" at a television screen. A good job I live on my own!

Please nod if *Question Time* causes a similar response from you (OK so I'm not the only one here who is bonkers/ OK so I do need to visit a psychiatrist)

One reason why we often delay switching off *Question Time*, persisting to the bitter end is that we want to see what the next question will be. Human beings, by nature, are curious, questioning creatures, always wanting to learn and discover more.

The Bible is full of questions. We started our service with three from Psalm 24:

"Who shall ascend the hill of the Lord?"
"Who shall stand in his holy place?"
"Who is the King of glory?"

Glance through the rest of the Psalms and you will easily spot that the remaining 149 of them are littered with questions directed by the worshipper at God. God is bombarded with human questions – reminiscent of a two year old child who is just discovering that the world around them is rather an interesting place. "Why do stars twinkle?" and, if you can manage to answer that one, invariably the child will ask "But why is it like that?"

"Why? How?......" We start asking questions at an early age and at some time we begin to wonder about God. The questions we all ask of God keep turning up in many of the Psalms.

Familiar ones such as:

"When I look at the heavens...the moon and the stars... Who are we that you should care for us?"

That's from Psalm 8 and two psalms later

"Why, O Lord, do you hide yourself in times of trouble?" (Ps.10)

In similar vein, "My God, Why have you forsaken me?" spoken by Jesus from the cross and found in Psalm 22.

"Why are you so cast down O my soul, And why are you so disquieted within me?"(Ps42)

Then to those big questions we all ask when we look at the wider world and see war, inequality and unfairness:

"Why do the nations so furiously rage together? and *"Why do the wicked prosper?"*

Familiar questions and we've only reached Ps 73.

It seems to me that the Psalms are full of trust (and lack of trust), of confidence (and fear), of affirmations of faith (and expressions of doubt), of adoring God (and complaining to him) and inevitably, of natural human questions which is why the Book of Psalms is very precious to Christians as well as to Jews. Here we have an important part of the scriptures which Jesus himself read and studied and loved.

Of course, the questions are not confined to the Psalms but are to be found in all parts of the Bible.

We can divide all our questions into two categories – human questions (that we ask of God) and divine questions (that God asks of us).

The latter is the subject and the title of a slim volume of sermons:

"Questions God asks us"

On the occasion of our Golden Wedding in 2009 we I received this book as a gift from some friends in South Africa. A welcome little present signed by the author Trevor Hudson at its book launch, with the inscription

"To Patricia and Brian with warm Christian South African greetings. God bless"

"Questions God asks us." Ten sermons, ten chapters from this Methodist minister. You will recognise some. They include the very first Bible question – the one asked by God in the Creation story which is widely recognised as a parable or myth but with powerful truths for all times, especially it seems for the 21st century with all *our* self-imposed problems.

Adam and Eve had broken the only rule they were given and had thus lost their closeness to God. In fear and shame they tried to hide in the bushes from their creator. But the Lord God called out to them,

"Where are you?"

It was the beginning of an estrangement, but also the start of the story of God's loving pursuit of his wayward children – a pursuit which continues through the Old Testament and (Christians believe) which is most clearly revealed in the New Testament in the life, death and resurrection of Jesus.

A further divine question from the Old Testament is in the story of the prophet Elijah, fleeing for his life from King Ahab and his very unfriendly wife Queen Jezebel. Elijah has taken refuge in a mountain cave, and there is a violent storm. The terrified prophet does not find God in the howling wind, or the flying rocks, nor in the earthquake or the flashes of lightning. It is in the ensuing sheer silence that the voice of God comes to him.

"What are you doing here Elijah?"

We capture that experience whenever we sing the hymn *"Dear Lord and Father of Mankind"*

*"Speak through the earthquake, wind and fire,
O still, small voice of calm!"*

God's calming words bring reassurance and hope to *us* as they did to Elijah – and the prophet was given one or two little extra jobs as well!

(God is like that, as you may have discovered!)

Into the New Testament Trevor Hudson's sermon title questions are the questions of Jesus. They include:

"Who do you say I am?" (to the disciples);

"Do you want to get well?" (to a paralysed man by Bethesda's Pool and to the broken hearted Mary Magdalene by the garden tomb), *"Why are you weeping?"*

You may have noticed that all of these questions contain the word YOU. They are all addressed by God or Jesus to the individual. In other words

*they are direct and personal.
They can be dodged or delayed,
but ultimately they demand an answer*

Whenever we turn to God we take the risk that God may respond by challenging us to be the answer to our own prayers and questions.

Jesus frequently responded to a question by *asking* another question, in effect saying "Well what do *you* think? Work it out!"

I want us now though to examine two really big questions, so part 2 of the sermon I call simply

"TWO REALLY BIG QUESTIONS"

We'll come to that in a moment but let's pause to sing a rather thought provoking hymn:

HYMN 644 *"When our confidence is shaken"*

Notice especially the exciting last verse which suggests that the answer to all our questions is in God. It is God's YES to our eternal WHY!

Let's sing, and think!

* * *

Readings: Mark 4 v.35-40

Mark 8 v.22-30

We have two really big questions there within four chapters of each other in St Mark's Gospel.

The first is a human question addressed to each other by the disciples after something extraordinary has happened to a raging sea.

The second is asked by Jesus of his disciples – and again remarkable things have been going on. (a blind man made to see) "Who is this man?" and "Who do *you* say I am?"

Both questions focus on Jesus and are two sides of the same coin really. Let's begin with "Who is this man?"

A few years ago, at a small village chapel in North Yorkshire, the distinguished preacher told us of how he had been invited to preach a sermon at an important service at Manchester University to be attended by students and learned professors and scholars in their different disciplines. "A prestigious occasion," he mused, "I'd better get this right!" So in the following weeks he took himself off to libraries and consulted great tomes of philosophy, wisdom, and theology. The day came and the time in the service where he was led to the pulpit. He climbed the stairs and laid out his carefully prepared notes on the oak lectern, waiting for the hymn being sung to end.

Then he noticed a text carved into the top of the oak stand, as a reminder to preachers of their task. It was from St John's Gospel, chapter 12 – the request of some Greek enquirers to Philip, one of the disciples: "We would see Jesus." They had heard of Jesus and wanted Philip to introduce them to his master so they could discover for themselves whether what they had heard about Jesus was in fact true.

"We would see Jesus." A simple request making that preacher ask himself whether what he had written and was about to deliver would reveal much about Jesus to his eager listeners. In dismay he concluded "Not a lot really." Then with great courage he put his sermon script aside and proceeded to speak from the heart about what Jesus meant to *him*, and how being a modern follower of Jesus had changed and *was* changing his life.

I suspect that his impromptu sermon probably touched more lives than his intellectual thesis would have done. I cannot imagine *I* would be brave enough to make such a last minute change.

Opinions will differ over what had happened to the terrified disciples in their fragile boat and to the powerful sea beneath and all around them.

Did Jesus really command the wind and the waves o suddenly go calm? Did he thereby perform a miracle over nature? (thus contradicting his temptations in the wilderness where he refused to use his powers to persuade people that he was the Messiah)

Or was the peace, the sudden calm, an internal one replacing the disciples' anxious fears with trust and faith and the strength to conquer their current troubles?

Or was it a mixture of both? Who knows and ultimately does it really matter, and should it trouble us? To get bogged down in such details makes us lose sight of the key question the first readers of Mark's Gospel all those centuries ago – and we today – are challenged to reach a decision about.

What impact does Jesus make on YOU and on the world?

"WHO IS THIS MAN?"

We may not know about storms on Galilee but each and every one of us is affected by stormy, worrying periods in our personal lives and crises in the world.

Could it be that we too, like those baffled and amazed disciples, could engage with this really big question "Who is this man who has the power to bring calm to our anxious lives?"

The disciples who first asked "Who is this man?" shared their opinions and strengthened each other. We too must lean upon the friendship of fellow Christians and the community of the church – of whom Jesus is Lord and as we sing, "Our sure foundation"

You will note that the question, "Who is this man?" is in the present tense and it will remain like that always, from generation to generation.

For many years in my classroom at the school where I taught Religious Studies I kept two books side by side on the shelf behind my desk.

One had the title "Jesus of History" and the other was called "Jesus Today".

I would sometimes tell pupils that this was unique to Jesus. No other historical person could be described in both past and present tenses. For instance you would not find books called "Churchill of History" and "Churchill Today". But with Jesus it's different.

Historians agree that two thousand years ago a Jew called Jesus walked through the villages and towns of his country teaching about life and God, that miracles of healing were attributed to him, that he attracted a number of followers, that he fell foul of the religious authorities and was put to death by Roman crucifixion.

People may deny the claims which Christians make about Jesus but scholars do not deny his existence. The author H.G.Wells, not himself a Christian, wrote this:

"An historian like myself, with no theological bias whatever, cannot portray the progress of humanity honestly without giving Jesus foremost place."

It is like seeing the wake of a huge ship. The vessel itself has gone out of our sight, but the waves, the aftermath, are sufficient for us to conclude that something really big has produced this effect.

Around 40 years ago someone, (we don't know who) reached *this* conclusion about Jesus:

> *"I am well within the mark when I say*
> *that all the armies that ever marched,*
> *and all the navies that ever sailed,*
> *and all the parliaments that ever sat,*
> *and all the kings that ever reigned,*
> *put together, have not affected the life of*
> *man upon earth as has that One Solitary Life.*

Soon after the crucifixion Christians began to go beyond the boundaries today laid down by historians as primary, concrete evidence, by entering the realms of faith, claiming that Jesus was more than just a remarkable man from Nazareth – that in fact Jesus fulfilled Jewish prophecies of a Messiah, who conquered death, and who is worthy of worship and of titles such as Son of God, Redeemer and Lord, and Saviour of the World.

More than that, Christians began to claim *(and still claim)* that Christ's death was somehow for the whole world, every single human being – which makes it intimately personal. Further still (and here's the unfathomable contradiction – or the amazing truth!), there was, and still is, the claim (as we shall soon sing) that Christ is no longer confined to distant years in Palestine. Rather, we claim that he is alive in the here and now, that he can be known in our daily lives, that he is suffering still in all the mess human beings make, and that in that involvement he is still being crucified. Yet he is for ever alive, and for ever offering us joy, justice, love: making him forever worthy of our praise and worship.

And that is why we come to church.

It's part of a lifelong quest to discover answers to those two really big questions "Who is this man?" and "Who do you think I am?"

I sign off with an illustration from that "Jesus Today" book resting on my classroom shelf all those years ago. It tells of two men who were looking round an old mosque in Istanbul. When first built it had been a Christian church but its Muslim successors had painted over all the Christian pictures and symbols when converting it into a place for their worship.

Now, centuries later, the paint was flaking off and the original pictures were becoming visible again. The two men looked up at the great dome where they could just make out through the flaking paint a large portrait of Jesus, with hands stretched out in blessing.

"You see," said one of the men turning to his friend, "He's coming back! You can't blot him out! Across the centuries he always comes back!"

I would want to add that in actual fact he has never gone away – which is why the question of those awe struck fishermen disciples, "Who is this man?" remains forever in the present tense and which is why Jesus's "Who do *you* say I am?" is as relevant now as it was when first asked.

(Preached at Wesley Road Ecumenical Chapel Leeds 12 on 19th July 2012)

CHAPTER 9

YES GOD IS GOOD!

If you want a title for this sermon it's in the opening words of a hymn which regularly was sung in Harvest Festival services but for some reason has not made it into "Singing the Faith."

"Yes, God is good – in earth and sky,
From ocean depths and spreading wood
Ten thousand voices seem to cry
'God made us all, and God is good!'"
(How many of you have sung it?)

Yes God is good! Most of us here this morning will agree with that sentiment. It is after all in *many* of our hymns and worship songs and throughout the Bible. But what do the words mean?

In what way is God good and how do we define goodness anyway? In your opinion and from your life's experiences how do you put into words God's so called goodness? What ideas come to mind when you think of the goodness of God? If say a friend or a child were to ask you "How is God good?" where might you begin to reply? (Think about that for a minute).

How vague that little adjective "good" is! In *non religious* everyday speech it can mean so many things. "How are you today?" we ask. "I'm good." The reply may be. We talk about a good book or film or TV programme, a good friend, good food. The word good can mean different things to different people. To some Donald Trump would be a good president whilst others think he is a disaster waiting for an opportunity.

In the world of our national *politics* views of what is good and what isn't become even *more* polarized – as issues like Brexit, the Northern Power House and our national rail service clearly demonstrate.

In *religious language* our focus is on spiritual qualities – but that doesn't make the use of the word good any easier.

Love, truth, beauty, perfection, holiness, fairness, greatness, power, justice are the sort of words we use when talking about God or addressing him in our prayers.

When our Muslim friends finger their prayer rosaries with 33 beads they are thinking of the 99 names for Allah (God) found in the Qur'an – which are actually descriptions of the many different facets or qualities of God: 99 names or attributes, one of which is goodness!

No wonder the simple word "good", when applied to God, is so deliberately vague, seemingly so inadequate, but also (please note) so invitingly embracing. God, after all is, and will remain, an exciting mystery, whose depths we are each invited to plumb, and whose love and friendship he would have us welcome and explore.

And that is the very best of the good news which Christians call the Gospel.

"Yes God is good!" is an expression of conviction and joy and eagerness.

YES!! is one of those capital letter responses with exclamation marks. It's not unlike when England, (or your favourite team) score a goal and you see the crowd raising their hands and you hear the united chorus, "Yes!"

(That, incidentally, is how we should say most of our Amens in church.)

To stretch the metaphor even further. Fellas, imagine you are a young man. Not so easy, perhaps, when we look in a mirror first thing in a morning or when we feel past our sell by date, but within each of us there still beats the heart of a younger self. So suspend reality for a few seconds and give way to imagination and there you are, standing before the most beautiful girl in the world with your heart a flutter and a little box in your hand. You have rehearsed the precious words but are still afraid of fluffing your lines or falling over when you try to kneel.

"Will you marry me?"

You would want the reply to be a firm and clear "Yes." A reluctant fumbled answer would be a bit disconcerting. Even more devastating to your ego would be a delayed "I'll think about it" or "I'll see what my mum says" or worst of all, "Not on your life. Stand up and get on yer bike!"

Yes is a lovely word then and all of us will have said it in more than one situation in our lives. And for the Christian or Jew, Hindu, Muslim or Sikh we will all have thought or voiced our assent that "Yes! *God is* good," thereby indicating that this feeling of gratitude and praise gives us inspiration and hope, - and a message to share.

I am certain that the writers of our hymns this morning thought so too, otherwise they wouldn't have produced such words as:

"Sing of the Lord's goodness"
And *"I sing the goodness of the Lord,*
That filled the earth with food;
He formed the creatures with his word,
And then pronounced them good."

Then that lovely idea from The Message version of Psalm 103 that the Lord "wraps us in his goodness."

But now for the practical bit. (Preaching should lead to practice, and listening to doing. Otherwise it's just words, words, words.) So let's go on to consider how we can live lives which will reflect this "goodness of the Lord"? about which I am (inadequately) trying to preach. But I'll come back to that later. Let's take a break now to make our offering during which we remain seated to sing and reflect on the hymn, "When all your mercies, O my God, my rising soul surveys…"

Hymn STF 97 (tune ii)

* * *

Back to the practical bits!

This is a packet of Triple A batteries.

It's a good idea to always keep some spares in your bits and bobs drawer at home. Keep them handy. You never know when you will need them because you never know when your TV handset will stop working or your clock hands will come to a halt, your computer mouse will run out of juice or your torch will not light up.

Metaphorically each one you is a triple A battery (and me). Some of you are super charged. (remember the Duracell longer life advert – always on the go, endless energy.)

The rest of you, I suspect, are just like me.

We can't keep up – but we just plod on. That makes us important because God needs plodders.

I suppose I could have made you any sort of battery but I chose to make us all triple A's (and let's be rechargeable) because 3A's lead to a three point sermon – a custom going back to a 4th century famous preacher St John Chrysostom, Bishop of Constantinople.

Three qualities, each beginning with the letter A, for us to cherish and take on board in our attempt to live a meaningful and authentic Christian life.

Three verbs, all starting with an A.

The FIRST is ACCENTUATE or, as the Disney film "Jungle Book" puts it, Accentuate the Positive – sung by an ape or gorilla which is why I'm wearing my monkey tie this morning. (Don't worry I'm not going to sing the song or swing from the lights.

Daily we are bombarded with so much negativity from the news media and from strangers, and friends – people whose glass always seems to be half empty rather than half full, always looking on the dark side, always complaining, demanding their rights whilst failing to mention their responsibilities. Mona Lotts we would call them, spreaders of gloom.

As Christians, one of our roles in life is to spread joy and happiness. "Always look on the bright side," to quote another popular old song.

Not always easy to do but even in the direst of circumstances there can be found a glimmer of hope, some lesson to be learned, if we positively look for it. Maybe every cloud *does* have a silver lining somewhere.

Another hymn which did not transfer from Hymns and Psalms to Singing the Faith has within it memorable lines such as:

"My God I thank thee, who has made the Earth so bright, so full of splendour and of Joy, beauty and light...

"I thank thee Lord that thou hast made joy to abound, so many gentle thoughts and deeds circling us round; that in the darkest spot on earth some love is found.

"I thank thee too that often joy is touched with pain. That shadows fall on brightest hours, that thorns remain, so that earth's bliss may be our guide and not our chain."

St Paul puts it well:

"All things work together for good for those who love God" Romans 8 v.28 – one of those bible verses worth storing in your memory bank of valuable treasures.

Which pushes us on to the SECOND of our Capital A verbs. Having learned to accentuate the positive we need to ANTICIPATE the good things, – but also the not so good things which we as human beings will have to deal with.

God's goodness is pleasant and wonderful to contemplate. It is grand and uplifting for us to count our blessings, to name them one by one as the old chorus has it (you may be singing it in your heads now). And it's true that when we do begin to count our blessings it may well surprise us to realise what the Lord has done.

But life is not all a bed of roses is it and becoming a Christian or a regular churchgoer doesn't mean that your problems will disappear. Acquiring faith in God is *not* an insurance policy to prevent bad things happening in your life.

The bible is very realistic about the place of suffering in the world and in the lives of believers. To become a Christian is not to escape from it, but to learn how to be able to bear the pain of distress, both physical and emotional, with dignity and hope.

On the final night of Jesus's life after the last supper in the charged atmosphere of the upper room, Jesus gave his disciples encouragement and warnings. They didn't understand all of what he said but they hung on every word.

Jesus spoke about joy and the Holy Spirit. There was much to give them strength and courage. But he also said this:

"In the world you will face trouble but fear not. I have conquered the world...As the father has loved me so I have loved you..

In me you will find peace... Abide in my love so that my joy may be in you and your joy may be complete..."

Anticipate the blessings then, which are free and abundant from the hands of a merciful and loving God, but be aware of and alert to the difficulties and challenges which are part of life – the temptations, our failings and mistakes, the breakdown of trust in relationships with family and friends, the loss of loved ones, the stutters in our career plans and in our health. None of us is immune to times when things go wrong in our lives. Such crises throw us off course and may lead to wobbles in our trust in God.

I think of the Old Testament character Job, a really good man, in the wonderful tale about the problem of suffering. Job lost family, cattle, wealth, everything dear to him and now even his health. So-called comforters told him that his misfortunes must be a punishment for sin. Job rejected this accusation and refused to accept the invitation to renounce his faith, declaring, "Even if God were to slay me I would still worship him." How many of us could stand with Job in such dire straits? Our crises are surely insignificant in comparison to Job's. So much so that when we are in danger of becoming a Mona Lot over little things maybe we need to rediscover our sense of humour. "Laughter is the best medicine," they say – and sometimes it is, especially if we can learn to laugh at ourselves.

If you want a good laugh and a good read, try getting hold of one of Fanny Flagg's novels.

She writes about life in small towns in the mid American state of Missouri in the second half of the 1900s. In one called "Standing in the Rainbow" she devotes a couple of chapters to Mrs Tot Whooten.

Poor Tot had a miserable childhood and as an adult she reflects that things have gotten even worse. She's always been at her family's beck and call, without much thanks. Now looking after grandchildren she is coughing up cash for her now grown up family despairing at her son's drug habits and consequent lack of work.

There was a ray of hope when her drunken husband had finally heeded the doctor's warnings and given up drinking. Now a seemingly reformed character he announced that for the first time in his life he was really in love. Tot's sudden glimmer of hope though was snuffed out when he revealed that the person he was in love was not herself but a flighty 20 year old girl from around the corner. So he left his wife.

Tot had reached rock bottom. She shut herself in her house, cutting off all connection with family and friends. She found it easy to just stay in bed most of the time, letting her house and well kept garden go to ruin. The concern of her neighbours fell on deaf ears. Peeping through her curtains one afternoon she spied her friend getting wrapped up in a line of drying sheets. Tot smiled but then found herself chuckling and finally laughing out loud at the growing chaos outside.

Do we (at least sometimes), need to avert our attention away from our own troubles, to relax a bit more, to look on the bright side, and to smile?

Now, there will be bumpy bits in the road ahead for each one of us. Part of our cure may be in our own hands but we have to heed the advice which Jesus gave to his disciples in the Upper Room and which he gives to us, his disciples in the 21st century:

be prepared, be alert, but be aware of the strength which God gives. In a single word; ANTICIPATE. And we can all do that by observing our third triple A battery verb which is ACCEPT. This is simple and so I can be brief.

Acceptance is all a matter of trust really. First we have to trust the numerous promises from God throughout the scriptures and especially in the words of Jesus. God, Jesus, the Holy Spirit are not liars. It is clearly evident from the scriptures and from people's testimonies that God in his grace accepts human beings,- _accepts us_ - just as we are, warts and all.

By circumstance of birth perhaps, *we* have been called to accept Jesus as Saviour and Lord and he accepts us. We respond to being so accepted by accepting one another and we should go on to accept those who, by chance of birth, belong to other faiths. We all worship the one God and Father of all humankind.

I fondly remember a magic moment from 20 years back. We had been invited to a friend's Big 0 birthday party held in a country park Christian conference centre near Sheffield.

We gathered in a large hall for fun and games.

At one point, out of the blue, my Big 0 friend Margaret introduced me and invited me to come and say a prayer. I went to the front to a large carpet where all the small children were sitting reading, drawing and colouring. I stood amongst them, closed my eyes and nervously began to pray. Suddenly I felt a small hand slip into mine. It was my grand daughter Bethany's hand almost as if she were saying, "Hello grandad. You'll be OK." It displayed her complete trust in me – and it was lovely.

Do you remember the small children in *your* life holding *your* hand. What a privilege it is to be so trusted! And that's how it is between God and us. We trust God and he trusts us. It's a hand in hand relationship. We are accepted!

A great German scholar and theologian was once asked what was the heart of his belief. He replied with words of the children's hymn:

"Jesus loves me this I know, for the bible tells me so."

Simply, that's all we need to know.

That's my finishing point but actually it's the starting point for us all.

To sum up:

>Accentuate all the positive blessings God provides.

>Anticipate that negative obstacles will arise but that God will help you in your times of need.

>Above all accept that God loves you.

>Remember finally that batteries can and do go flat. We, Triple A's, need regular recharges.

But that's another sermon and anyway here we are, worshipping together – and that's a very important habit, and a commendable way to start any new week.

Have a good one!

See you (be here) next Sunday, same time, same place, same happy, smiling faces!

CHAPTER 10

THE CROSS: TRAGEDY AND TRIUMPH

Lower Wortley Methodist Leeds 12 Passion Sunday 29th March 2009

"When I am lifted up from the earth," Jesus said, "I will draw everyone to me." (John 12v.32). Words used on two other occasions in John's Gospel sometimes referring to Jesus being lifted up into glory, as at the Ascension, but here specifically applied to his being lifted up on the cross.

On Passion Sunday we begin to focus on the suffering and death of Jesus – a process which takes us through Palm Sunday's defiant and courageous entry into the cauldron of Jerusalem's Passover preparations and on to the events of what we call Holy Week, culminating in the Last Supper, the agony in Gethsemane, the betrayal, arrest, beating and humiliation and finally the cruel indignity of public execution: a slow and painful death on a Roman cross.

I read somewhere about a small girl being taken to a church service for the first time. The gospel reading was one of the accounts of Jesus's crucifixion. At the end of the service, as they were leaving, her mother noticed that tears were streaming down her daughter's cheeks.

"Why did they kill him?" the child sobbed. "And why is nobody else crying?" The continuation of the story was apparently not known to her, but for us the question remains – why doesn't the crucifixion of Jesus disturb and upset us more than it does?

I watch an appeal from the NSPCC on the TV and I could cry; I see pictures of starving children and dying women in Sudan's refugee camps and choke back the tears; I read a novel or watch a film portraying deep sorrow and loss and find myself welling up. Yet I can read or hear the story of the brutal treatment and ugly death of the One alone whom I am happy to claim, "He is my Friend and my Saviour," and I find myself comparatively unmoved.

Why should this be when I love Jesus and I know even more surely that he loves me? Is it because I have heard the story so many times that familiarity has bred, not contempt, but a measure of indifference?

Is it because I already know that Easter Day follows Good Friday and there is a gloriously happy ending?

Is it because it all happened so long ago that it has lost its immediacy and has become just one more tragic event in a whole quagmire of terrible suffering and wrongs which humanity has inflicted on innocent victims down the centuries?

Or is it because maybe my walk with God is not as close to him as it used to be and I sometimes echo the hymn writer's words: "Where is the blessedness I knew when first I saw the Lord?" (461 MHB "O for a closer walk with God")

These questions I have to ask of myself. Do you?

We need to look again and keep reminding ourselves of the significance of the cross, trying to understand something of what it meant for Jesus and what it means for us and the world – though of course we shall never fully plumb the depths of this act of divine love. But let's at least try, and what better Sunday is there than Passion

Sunday to make an attempt? How might we proceed?

The first of two steps we could take is for us to **focus on the cross and recognise the tragedy of it.**

During the season of Lent many churches, across the denominations, have adopted the custom of transforming a cross. The whole process is poignant and full of meaning. The cross is sometimes made from the previous year's Christmas tree and stands in a prominent position at the front of the church. On each of the six Sundays in Lent a symbolic reminder of the objects which played a part in the crucifixion is placed by the tree. First 30 silver coins calling to mind the betrayal of Jesus, then a cup, for the Last Supper, next a whip for the scourging, then a purple cloak, followed by a crown of thorns and finally three large nails.

Step by step the relentless and dramatic path to the cross is traced and we are made to feel the tension building up for Jesus and his disciples. We try to imagine ourselves actually present during that time.

Then comes Easter Sunday morning and we enter the church to find that somebody has been busy and the bare wooden cross is filled with spring flowers transforming it from an object of ugliness and shame into something beautiful. So we rejoice that our Lord has conquered death and the grave, bringing to the world new life, hope and possibilities of a fresh loveliness.

The whole ceremony of the Lenten Cross is one which I value, but I have to admit that there is one part of it which troubles me and which I have not yet resolved. The question I have is this:

*Can we **ever** transform the cross into something beautiful? Must it not remain what it was at the time and will always be – an instrument of execution? (with the added deterrent of public humiliation). There is nothing beautiful about that, especially if the crucified one is blameless and a victim of jealousy, hatred and injustice.*

Jesus was transformed, not the cross, which was probably used again, and again and yet again.

And it is **lives that can be transformed** when people come to realise something of what Jesus accomplished for them on the cross and that in some inexplicable way he suffered and died for **them**, for **their** sins, to bring them forgiveness, and God's friendship eternally. (and the *them* includes you and me)

The cross was not transformed, but we continue to adorn our churches with splendid crosses because the cross has become a powerful symbol of Christianity. Some would say that the cross is at the *centre* of our faith, but doesn't that statement switch the emphasis away from the crucified Lord?

He is at the heart of our faith, not the cross upon which he died! Indeed the Apostle Paul himself, writing to the Corinthians claims that he has been sent to proclaim the Good News of the gospel and to make sure that Christ's death on the cross is not robbed of its power. (1 Cor 1v.23). We preach a crucified Lord.

Many churches prefer a cross without the dying or dead body of our Lord pinned to it because, as the hymn says:

"Christ is alive! Let Christians sing;
His cross stands empty to the sky." (HP190)

Wearing an empty cross on a gold chain round the neck can be a witness leading into conversation, as some of you will testify, but there must be many who see it just as a piece of jewelry without thinking about its significance. If you don't know who it stands for then you might just as well wear a set of hangman's gallows or an electric chair round your neck!

The cross was used by the Romans for killing criminals and as such, especially in the case of Jesus, it always was full of tragedy. **Focus on the cross and *recognise* the tragedy** of it.

Down the centuries many attempts have been made to try to explain why Jesus died. Theories of the atonement they are called. None of them is entirely satisfactory; some indeed are quite repellant to modern minds. We come across them in some of the earlier hymns – such as the cross being a remedy for Adam and Eve's sin which tainted us all; or a necessary ransom being paid to God or Satan.

We might still sing some of these hymns but at the back of our minds is the thought that biblical scholarship and theology have moved on since then. However, when such ideas linger on into modern hymns and songs it is less palatable.

"In Christ alone" is a lovely hymn but for the life of me I cannot sing the lines which state that "on the cross as Jesus died the wrath of God was satisfied." To my way of thinking if you say that the cross was God's intention and his way of appeasing his anger for our sins then it makes the death of Jesus even more tragic than it actually was.

Whatever was achieved by the cross surely it was a tragedy that this good man died in such a cruel way. And if you push the Father and Son analogy to its limits then this crucifixion is a tragedy, not only for Jesus and humanity, but also for God himself, especially if you dare to entertain the shocking conclusion that God (the Father) planned the death of Jesus (his Son), or stood by doing nothing to prevent it. If God was *powerless* to stop it then try to imagine *his* grief. Which ever way you look at this the cross was, and still is, an immeasurable tragedy.

> *"See from his head, his hands, his feet,*
> *Sorrow and love flow mingled down;*
> *Did e'er such love and sorrow meet.*
> *Or thorns compose so rich a crown?"*

Tragedy! Nothing less than sheer tragedy! The world was bruised on that day by this event. But out of that tragedy there came forth something quite remarkable –

as hopefully we shall see, after we have sung that hymn by Isaac Watts:

HP 180 *"When I survey the wondrous cross"*

Whilst we must ever recognise the tragedy of the cross we must also never cease to **rejoice in the triumph of the cross,** and that's the other point I want to make.

That triumph is perfectly illustrated in the Church's ancient collect for Passion Sunday. Let's pray that prayer now:

"Most merciful God, who by the death and resurrection of your Son Jesus Christ delivered and saved the world: grant that by faith in him who suffered on the cross, we may triumph in the power of his victory; through Jesus Christ our Lord, who is alive and reigns with you, in the unity of the Holy Spirit, one God, now and for ever. Amen."

For the mother of Jesus, and the handful of loyal friends gathered round the cross watching the writhing body of Jesus and trying to catch his every last word as he slowly and painfully slipped away from them, the tragedy of all this must have broken their hearts. Neither could the frightened disciples who had turned and fled escape the inconsolable grief of what had happened.

Even on the Sunday morning, a couple of days later, Mary Magdalene in the garden at the tomb, is still crying. "Why are you weeping?" the angels ask her. Moments later the risen Jesus repeats the question, "Why are you weeping?" though she mistakes him for the gardener.

"Mary!" says Jesus – and the seemingly impossible truth dawns. Jesus has come back to life!

The tragedy of the cross has not been eliminated. It never can be. Mary saw Jesus die and that crushing memory, with all the heartbreak it brought, was burned deeply into her whole being.

But now the time for grieving has gone because after the tragedy of the cross comes the triumph of resurrection from the grave. Don't let us confine triumph to the resurrection though because triumphs had already been won on the cross. It is finished!" Jesus had cried out before he died – in the sense of "It is accomplished; it is done!" Such a shout of triumph suggests that his victories were won on the cross, and sealed by God three days later when he raised him from death. The ultimate victory over the grave !

Somehow or other, known to God alone, but guessed at by scholars and theologians and preachers ever since Jesus died, God turned the tragedy of the cross into a victory, and the triumph of the cross is far greater than its tragedy could ever be – though both remain.

Which is why, of all the world's great religions, Christianity alone has an instrument of execution as its symbol, for in the suffering, dying Jesus we see a number of triumphs:

the victory of love over hatred,
of good over evil,
of gentleness over anger,
of courage over cowardice,
of self sacrifice over self preservation.

Whilst we must always recognise the *tragedy* of the cross we must also never cease to rejoice in the *triumphs* of the cross.

Shall I tell you the really good news though? The really good news is that they are triumphs freely given by God to all of us, including you and me, for us to accept, savour and enjoy.

They tell us that God loves us personally,

that Jesus died for us,

that he wants us to turn to him

so that he can welcome and forgive us,

and so that we can share all his wonderful goodness today, tomorrow, next week, next month,

for the rest of our lives and eternally.

I finish with some afterthoughts, used by me in a Good Friday Service of meditations some years ago.

Time travel

How many of you watch the Dr Who dramas?

I've always been fascinated with the idea of time travel. That doesn't automatically turn me into a Dr Who fan especially when the good Time Lord journeys into the future. How could you go forward to a time which has not yet happened?

Neither am I a Star Trekker, though those programmes do raise some quite deep moral and philosophical issues.

Going *back* in time has got its problems. Wouldn't that interfere with what happened and what has been recorded about such events ever since? Much as we would like sometimes, we can't alter history. If only we could!

Still the idea of time travel remains interesting to me, even though I recognise it as fantasy – science fiction not science fact. Which is why a short story from a newspaper competition some years ago appeals to me It is about a family sometime in the future who decide to go on a time travel holiday. After much consideration they decide to travel back in time to see the crucifixion of Jesus. (It was printed in my book "Inside the Preacher's Mind " in the chapter "Let's Go to Golgotha".)

We would probably decline to sign up for any such trip even if it were possible but in in a sense we are still involved because the hatred and cruelty and all the sins which helped to crucify Jesus are still around today, in spite of this Good Man's courage, love, example and teaching.

People have not listened to Jesus, or do not understand his message of love and forgiveness. But Christians do, so whenever we hear again the story of the crucifixion or sing about it in our hymns let us try to understand that in his death Jesus was, and is, somehow saying to each one of us "See how much I love you!" And his resurrection confirms his love for us each day and FOR EVER.

CHAPTER 11

CALLED TO BE SAINTS
(or friends on earth and friends above)

At the end of a busy day I often relax by looking for a light hearted TV comedy sitcom and so, recently, I found myself watching an episode of "Last of the Summer Wine".

It was a lesson in how to remember your wife's birthday and what to do if you forget. Howard had forgotten to buy a present for his fearsome wife Pearl. He went to seek advice from his neighbour – who was not in. On the table was what appeared to be a large box of chocolates, all neatly wrapped and ribboned. "I'll borrow these," said Howard and trotted off back home not knowing that the pretty box contained not chocolates but a dead ferret prepared for burial in the church graveyard. As usual the three well-meaning but meddlesome men had got it all wrong and their efforts to put things right only made matters much worse.

Whilst there are certain things in our lives we would like to forget there are other dates and events which are essential for us to remember. The latter are far more important.

In a field near Lee Abbey in Devon (a Christian conference centre) there is a sign which reads something like this: "On the 1st of April 1786 on this very spot, nothing happened."

The 21st October 2015 had television interviewers on the streets asking people if they knew the significance of that day. Few folk knew that it was the date set in Doc Brown's time machine – a super modified DeLorean sports car catapulted into the future way back in 1955. You will tell me the name of the highly successful film and its sequels:

BACK TO THE FUTURE

Back to the future is of course a contradiction in terms, but is it, I wonder, in some ways a possible reality?

It is said that the people of Pisa with its leaning towers in Italy were asked why there was no clock on their tower. The reply was, "We had the inclination but we just didn't have the time."

Is that the answer we sometimes give to God? There is a job to be done at church and we have all the skills needed. Out come our excuses, Our time is free but where is our inclination? "Here I am Lord. Please ask someone else," is often our first response.

Come with me in your imagination to a Sunday morning service in the Greek city of Corinth nearly 2000 years ago, round about 53 AD. We are in the room of a larger than usual house where a small group of Christians are meeting early to worship together before their day's work begins. There are no New Testament Scriptures to listen to because the Gospels have not yet been written, but there are prayers and stories of Jesus which have been passed down from previous generations.

Worship is always exciting but today there is a special buzz because a letter has been received from the Apostle Paul and is to be shared with them. The scroll is unrolled and the reader begins. All eyes are fixed on him. Everyone is very attentive and eager not to miss a single word. So they drink in Paul's opening greetings which we can find in his first letter to the Corinthians, chapter 1 v.1-9.

Try to capture at least some of their pent up anticipation as they hear these word of Paul:

"Paul, called to be an apostle of Christ Jesus by the will of God, and our brother Sosthenes, to the church of God that is in Corinth, to those who are sanctified in Christ Jesus, called to be saints...... grace to you and peace from God our Father and the Lord Jesus Christ.

I give thanks to my God always for you because of the grace of God that has been given you in Christ Jesus, for in every way you have been enriched in him, in speech and knowledge of every kind – just as the testimony of Christ has been strengthened among you – so that you are not lacking in any spiritual gift as you wait for the revealing of our Lord Jesus Christ."

The little congregation in Corinth must have been thrilled to hear so much praise. Hopefully they would accept with grace the wisdom and advice and criticism which was to follow, seeing them as God's Word not just Paul's words.

Every Sunday when we hear the words of scripture being read, it is a "back to the future moment" because the Word of God is not dead and dusty ancient history, of importance then but of no relevance for today. No! God's Word is a living word for all time – for the future which has now become our past, for the present day and for the ages still to come.

So we go back to the scriptures to find out what God said and to try to unravel what is his message for us today. Make no mistake, there are messages for us as there were messages for those Christians in Corinth all those centuries ago. Maybe there will be differences because of changing times and cultures, but it is still God's word that we may hear.

A few years ago I preached a sermon on that lovely story in Luke chapter 24 on the incident on the very first Easter evening where the risen Jesus walks with two followers on the Road to Emmaus. It is dusk; they are distraught at what has been done to Jesus on a criminal's cross, and they fail to recognise the stranger who tags along with them on their journey. It is only when they invite him into their home for supper and he breaks the bread that they realise he is Jesus – alive and back from the dead. And then Jesus vanishes and the two dash back to Jerusalem to share their tremendous news with the disciples.

This is one of my favourite gospel stories, and maybe yours too. I had always accepted it at face value as an accurate, historical account. But my research for the sermon revealed that there are huge question marks in the minds of scholars over lots of the details with indeed even the suggestion that the story may be an invention in the mind of an incredibly gifted and artistic writer.

We don't know for certain. It may have occurred just as written in every detail or it may be an embroidered telling of some chance encounter on that dusty road. We don't even know the name of one of the travellers and we can't call on television film recordings as evidence.

What we can point out however, and this I did, is that in one sense it doesn't matter. Rejecting its historical truth does not mean that you are denying or undermining your faith in, and your love for the risen Christ. As in lots of Bible stories the really important thing is to look for the deeper, symbolic meaning. In other words to always ask "What can I discover from this passage of scripture about Jesus, about God, about life?"

A renowned American theologian, John Dominic Crossan, comments on Luke's memorable account in two three word sentences: "Emmaus never happened. Emmaus always happens. Going back to the past we learn about our present – about what God may be doing, and can do today. Going back to the future can be very revealing and rewarding.

So what can we learn for today by going back to Paul's opening greetings in his letter to the Corinthians? I draw your attention to how Paul describes these Christians in Corinth. He refers to them as "those who are sanctified in Christ Jesus, called to be saints," and if he were to address us it would be the same. We here in Armley, Leeds, a small group of Christians met together for worship, are sanctified in Jesus and called to be saints.

The word saint can be a bit misleading. It conjures up images of stained glass window figures and haloes, of heroic lives or grim deaths, of unbelievable piety and prayerful attitudes. We wouldn't want to be like that!

Such veneration is an invention of the church as it developed during the centuries after the Apostle Paul. Maybe he would have been horrified to learn that one day he would be referred to as "Saint" Paul!

The Greek word Paul uses here is *hagios,* meaning set apart, different, special. When Paul speaks of the saints in Christ Jesus, as he often does, he means those who are different from other people because they have willingly entered into a relationship with Jesus: they recognise his importance, they experience his love, they try to live out his teachings , they worship him, they talk to him. What he said and did makes sense and he becomes an influence for good on their lives.

The Christians at Corinth were no doubt bolstered by Paul's kind and loving greetings but Paul was to pull no punches. As they continued to listen some of them would feel very uncomfortable because he told them straight what he thought of certain aspects of their behaviour. They were not saints with a capital S. (as you will see if you read it for yourself) They were saints of the rank and file, ordinary folk like us, who blow hot and cold, who lose heart sometimes and make bad decisions, who still have a lot to learn and a long way to go in our discipleship. They and we are after all saints with a small "s", who will never hit the headlines but who nonetheless are capable of being a great influence on the lives of others.

There is a lot of encouragement and teaching in this letter and Paul's final message is another bit of "back to the future" advice for us today when he says to both Corinthian and Armley Christians:

"Keep alert, stand firm in your faith, be courageous, be strong. Let all that you do be done in love."

I know a few details of some of the canonised and glorified Saints of the Church, but we can never meet them because the recognition and exaltation of such men and women is a complicated and lengthy process not completed until long after they have died. We cannot know personally these capital "S" Saints, but most of us, perhaps all of us, can bring to mind small "s" saints. These are people whose love and faith have made our lives richer, some of whom we could call friends.

"For the beauty of the earth" is a favourite hymn of mine, especially its mention of friends who enrich us: friends on earth, still alive, and friends above whom we have known and loved, and who have helped us to be better people. Please let me share a few memories of my friends, my saints with a small "s".

I suppose that my first faltering steps towards a Christian faith came at the age of seven or eight when I started going to Sunday School at Bramley Ebenezer Methodist Church in Leeds. Perhaps it was there that

I picked up the habit of saying my prayers every night – though they were somewhat trite and perfunctory: "Thank you God for today Sorry for the wrong things I've done. Bless mam and dad and brother and sister and give me a good night's sleep. Amen!" Some Sunday School teacher at Bramley Ebenezer (an unknown saint, I don't know who) must have encouraged us to talk to God.

We used to go into church for the first ten minutes of the service and one preacher (again I don't know who) told us that in our own prayers we should always say thank you to God for Jesus. Strange how that has stuck in my mind – or is it?

After a couple of years I transferred my allegiance to the Church of England, joining the choir at the Venerable Bede Church where I picked up my love for hymns, anthems and the chanting of the Psalms. We were paid a penny for each practice and service and a shilling when we sang at weddings. So it was rewarding in more ways than one, though I can't remember ever benefiting from the sermons – apart from improving my skills at doodling!

My voice broke and because I had school friends who went to the Youth Club at Wesley Road Methodists in Armley I again swapped sides, eventually getting involved in the Youth Fellowship and even teaching (very badly I suspect) in the Sunday School. We had a couple of Youth Leaders – Audrey Shepherd and Dorothy Ripley – both of whom were to become teachers at a missionary school in Nigeria.

They always finished Youth Club with an epilogue.

One, about prayer, I was to use on many an occasion in later years when I became an RE teacher.

John Egan, small in stature but large in heart, was another Wesley Road influence. A crowd of us teenagers used to meet in his flat. I never joined his Boys' Brigade but I enjoyed the young people's fellowship groups at his house. John also had a television – and that was an additional attraction!

Then came National Service and I found myself in Egypt and then in Cyprus. In Egypt I attended the MMG (Mission to Mediterranean Garrisons) run by three charming, (and to us), elderly ladies. Their kindness and caring, especially their Sunday lunches and Christmas parties brought a little bit of home to many a young soldier and airman feeling stranded in a land of sand, heat, barbed wire and flies.

The MMG hosted the usual fellowship meetings and a mid-week Gospel Service where regularly young lives were committed to Christ. Returning in an army truck from one such meeting in November 1954 we sang our choruses and praised God beneath a beautiful star filled sky. I was happy and uplifted. The following evening I went to a prayer meeting in one of the tents we lived in. Not many there, maybe half a dozen. John Mankey, (whose witness and testimony had impressed me), prayed. The humility in his prayer hit me. The previous night's praises did not evaporate but I found myself looking into my own life and seeing the need for forgiveness and commitment.

I guess that was a turning point – a moment in a conversion of some sort, though hardly dramatic. Nothing like the Damascus Road experience of Paul or the vivid "heart warming" of John Wesley in a room in Aldersgate Street London on the 24th May 1738 at a quarter to nine in the evening, but real enough for me to recall. John went on to become an Anglican vicar in Australia. He was unaware of the way God used him that evening but I am grateful that he was a significant milestone in my Christian pilgrimage.

There was also the free church in the garrison, St Mark's, where I worshipped on Sundays and helped in their Sunday School. I even went on a course about local preaching, run by a Methodist padre. It gave me a week's rest from office work and guard duties. We did have to write a sermon. Mine never reached a pulpit! The friendship of many fine young Christians in Egypt and Cyprus was such an influence and I remained in touch with some of them, That was a long time ago though and there's only me left of our close group.

At Episkopi in Cyprus , headquarters of the Middle East Land Forces, there was no MMG. There was, however, a free church with a very lively Church of Scotland Padre, John Murrie. John was great fun and he had a loud voice. One of his favourite hymns was "From sinking sands he lifted me." I can still hear his voice booming out as we sang the rousing chorus. Padre Murrie baptised me during one evening service. I had already been received into membership of the Methodist Church before I joined the army. My parents had Baptist links so I had not been "done" as a baby. John Murrie corrected the omission.

Other names from those National Service days include Peter Hopkins, who was to be Best Man at our wedding. I honestly believe that Peter was actually the best man it has been my privilege to know. Peter tragically died at the age of 33. He had burned himself out in serving Jesus through caring for others. It makes me happy to know that Peter and Margaret's eldest son, who is now a doctor in Sheffield, was named after me. There aren't many Brians around these days due perhaps to "The Magic Roundabout". How many parents would give their son the same name as a snail?

Then there was Robin McGlashan, who won boxing blues for both Oxford and Cambridge. I went to Evensong with him at Kings College in the advent after my demob. Robin became an Anglican priest. My wife Patricia and I visited him at Ormskirk when he became a curate but most of his ministry was spent in India, teaching New Testament Greek at the Tamil Nadu Theological College. On furlough once he came to stay with us and we went to hear him preach at Ripon Cathedral. Robin was also a qualified psychotherapist. We rarely met but I was always at ease with Robin even though he was streets ahead of me on an intellectual and theological level. We were army "muckers" who became soul mates. Robin died in 2012 – another name on my "friends above" list.

After demob I returned to Wesley Road full of enthusiasm. We started a weekly Scripture Union Bible Study and Prayer Meeting. We formed a Mission Band of young people taking services around the circuit, a number of whom were to become preachers and church leaders in various places.

My own call to be a local preacher came on a cold Sunday evening one January in the early 1960s. There was a sparse congregation in the vast Wesley Road church. The Revd Arthur Harris, who had a slow, deliberate preaching style spoke about the parable of the talents. "If you have a talent and you don't use it," he said, "you will lose it."

I realised then that I could no longer put off the challenge. Shortly after that I started local preacher training.

I skip through the years because of the time but I must mention the influence of Leeds West Circuit ministers David Sixsmith, Gordon Lister and Brian Edmundson – from whom I learned a lot about Christian living and preaching.

I carry Brian's memorial service picture in my hymn book and sometimes, during a service, I'll sneak a look and be encouraged by his smile and his unforgettable courage and faith. Brian knew how to preach. I've never been able to match the way he got his message across so effectively with such economy of words. And he knew how to face terminal illness. It was a salutary privilege for me as Circuit Steward, neighbour and friend to stand with Brian on the threshold of heaven during his last days on earth.

It's not just friends we have known personally who influence us is it? For me it has been women and men of great faith whose lives and ideas have touched me through books. But that's another sermon for another occasion.

I have shared with you some of my "Friends on earth and friends above" list. Thank you for letting me do that.

There will be many names on your list too and when we pause to think about them their overall impact on our lives is quite amazing.

Why should that be? Is it their personality, wisdom, faith, sense of fun, their caring that has affected us? Well yes it's a mixture of all those qualities. But is there something else? And is that hidden extra not some thing but rather some one?

In all these people I see Jesus because he dwells within and shines through those who commit their lives to him even though they may not be aware of it. The Holy Spirit works through us (sometimes in spite of us) to spread the love and power of Jesus. If you think about it that's quite amazing isn't it? And if you reflect further you may find yourself reaching the same conclusion that I do – that it is the love and friendship of lovely Christian friends and saints that first attracted me to the church and keeps me firmly within its fellowship.

Finally I must point out that although this sermon was first preached across in Armley, Leeds I have since come to live in Knutsford. I still retain friendships in Leeds of course but even in my eighties have made new friends in my new circuit and have been warmly welcomed. So when I referred earlier to God's Word being relevant for Corinth and Armley I can now easily add your churches and people whose warmth and friendliness I was beginning to experience before Covid-19 interrupted – Alderley Edge, Mobberley, Knutsford, Plumley and the churches I have not yet had the pleasure of sharing worship with.

May we all be enriched by each other and by our own special friends on earth and friends above. Remember Paul's words "We are sanctified in Christ Jesus and called by God to be saints."

Preached at Whingate Methodist Church Leeds 12 on All Saints Day 2006. Since revised on a number of occasions. Has not had an outing in the Alderley Edge Circuit